Praise for *Generosity Unbound*

"Claire Gaudiani has a well-earned reputation as one of the leading thinkers about American philanthropy. Here she analyzes the challenges of coming years and shows how we can unleash the full idealism and generosity of the nation. She has made yet another welcome contribution."

> —*David Gergen, Director, Center for Public Leadership,*
> *The Kennedy School, Harvard University*

"*Generosity Unbound* unmasks Gaudiani as an unreconstructed, unapologetic believer in the transformative potential of American-style philanthropy. Drawing on appeals to history, reason, pride, and passion, she invites us to envision a role for philanthropy that is worthy of its past. Gaudiani's 'Declaration Initiative' would commit philanthropy to a cause no less noble, ambitious, and essential than that of ending persistent poverty and, at long last, affording all Americans true access to the equal opportunity that lies at the core of the democratic ideal."

> —*Ralph Smith, Executive Vice President, The Annie E. Casey Foundation*

"Gaudiani presents a timely solution to the economic and political crises facing our nation. *Generosity Unbound* is a fresh look at America's philanthropic past and how private foundations can be the vanguard of a path back to prosperity—for those hit hardest by the recession, and for our entire nation."

> —*Edwin J. Feulner, Jr., President, The Heritage Foundation*

"Critics of wealthy foundations would do well to read Claire Gaudiani's powerfully argued defense of American philanthropic freedom. And those who wish to preserve this freedom would do well to consider her bold 'Declaration Initiative.' Let's see what entrepreneurial generosity can accomplish when mobilized around a set of goals consistent with this country's founding vision."

> —*J. Gregory Dees, Professor, Center for the Advancement of Social*
> *Entrepreneurship, Fuqua School of Business, Duke University*

"Claire Gaudiani shows eloquently that the generosity of the American people is rooted in our freedom and our freedom is rooted in our generosity. She issues a stirring call for new philanthropic leadership that will open the gates of opportunity for all Americans."

—*Adam Meyerson, President, Philanthropy Roundtable*

"While some would suggest that philanthropy is on its heels, Claire Gaudiani shows us the potential that America's philanthropic sector has to activate our country's moral leadership and unleash citizen generosity for the purpose of addressing our unfinished quest for justice for all."

—*Tracy Gary, author, and Founder, Inspired Legacies & The Progressive Legacy Project*

"Claire Gaudiani's *Generosity Unbound* is a welcome dose of 'common sense for the common good' of our nation. Her challenge to philanthropic leaders of all political stripes—left, right, and center—to gather around a shared goal of meaningful opportunity and prosperity for all Americans should be heeded. Perhaps philanthropy can model what too many of our political leaders seem to be unable or unwilling to do: construct a safe place where our nation's ideas are not needlessly trampled by ideologies."

—*Robert K. Ross, M.D., President and CEO, The California Endowment*

"*Generosity Unbound* shows how the philanthropic tradition is firmly rooted in American history and culture. It serves as a critical inspiration and challenge to today's leaders to preserve the freedom and opportunity that make this tradition a uniquely vibrant force for good in the world."

—*James Piereson, President, William E. Simon Foundation*

"In this vitally important book, Claire Gaudiani convincingly makes the case that philanthropy has the capacity—and must use it—to heal the divisions in our society and to advance a renewed and enduring commitment to social justice that meets the challenges of our times."

—*Stephen Heintz, President, Rockefeller Brothers Fund*

Generosity Unbound

Generosity Unbound

*How American Philanthropy
Can Strengthen the Economy and
Expand the Middle Class*

CLAIRE GAUDIANI

NEW YORK, NEW YORK

Gaudiani, Claire.
    Generosity unbound : how American philanthropy can strengthen the economy and expand the middle class / Claire Gaudiani. — New York, NY : Broadway Pub., c2010.

        p. ; cm.
        ISBN: 978-1-931764-18-6 (cloth) ; 978-1-931764-19-3 (pbk.)
        Includes bibliographical references and index.

        1. Generosity—United States. 2. Humanitarianism—United States—History. 3. United States—Economic conditions. 4. Charities—Economic aspects—United States. 5. Endowments—Economic aspects—United States. I. Title.

HV91 .G38 2010
361/.973—dc22   1009

Published by:
Broadway Publications
Institute for American Values
1841 Broadway, Suite 211
New York, NY 10023
www.americanvalues.org

Manufactured in the United States of America

For Francesca Socorro Burnett,
Consuelo Gaudes Burnett,
and Alexander Zalo Cakaj,
my grandchildren;
and for the grandchildren of all readers.

It is for them that all our work together to
advance justice, generosity, and the ideals of the
American Republic matters the most.

The core strength of American foundations
is not in the amount of money they give away but
in their Constitution-given right to disburse it with
absolute autonomy, subject only to non-substantive,
process-oriented legal restrictions. . . . The Supreme
Court has held that the spending of money by
individuals and by associations of individuals in
pursuit of sociopolitical ends is itself speech, and that
such spending through charitable donations and the
foundations created thereby is protected speech.

–Joel Fleishman,
The Foundation: A Great American Secret

TABLE OF CONTENTS

PART I
Generosity Unbound:
Citizen-to-Citizen Generosity in America

PART II
A Primer on American Generosity

PART III
Generosity Unbound:
A Proposal for a Declaration Initiative

ACKNOWLEDGMENTS

This book owes a great deal to a great many people. I accepted a fellowship at the Institute for American Values to research and write a book about challenges to America's traditions of citizen generosity because I believe so strongly in the power of these values. My personal commitments to alleviating poverty and discrimination strengthened my belief that state and/or federal legislation to prescribe such commitments would be the wrong way to realize the ideals of our Declaration of Independence. With the Institute's generous support, I stopped teaching and spent the past year focused on this problem. I am grateful to the Institute and to its formidable president, David Blankenhorn. I have had full authorial freedom to address the many contentious issues discussed in *Generosity Unbound*. The ideas in this book are fully my own and I take personal responsibility for them.

I am deeply grateful to the many members of the field of philanthropy who met with me before I began to write this book. They advised me on how I could address the concerns of the Greenlining Institute and the National Committee for Responsive Philanthropy while still reinforcing the importance of independence for America's foundations and their creators. Among these are Joel Fleishman, Mark and Ashley Berner, Steve Heintz, Paul Brest, and Ellen Friedman.

These colleagues and the generous readers of drafts enabled me to believe that guarding the freedom of private foundations was fully harmonious with advancing the opportunities of America's poorest and most excluded citizens. Moreover, I became convinced that on these issues, the labels of liberal and conservative do not necessarily distinguish agendas, goals, or commitments. I am most grateful for the courage I saw in those who could hold and commit to both ideas at the same time. Many readers from across the political spectrum graciously read every page and commented often. I am deeply grateful to each of them. They enabled me to hear many different voices on complex issues, make fewer factual errors, and include a more varied set of examples of the philanthropic progress underway in our vast country. Some of these generous readers include Edwin Feulner, Gina Shea, Michael Gilligan, Linetta Gilbert, James Piereson, Robert Ross, Adam Meyerson, Jessica Chao, Mark Berner and Ashley Rogers Berner, Franklin D. Gilliam, Jr.,

Sue Santa, William Massey, Miriam Shark, Mark Constantine, Sandra Swirski, and Stefan Pryor. Despite this fortunate gift of wise counsel, I have doubtless allowed faults to remain. For these I accept sole responsibility.

I want to thank the foundations and organizations that have worked for so many years to enrich our nation's commitment to justice, freedom, education, health, science, the arts, and the spirit of idealism that still permeates the United States. America must rely on trust and generosity from private philanthropy if it is to remain the nation that is fulfilling age-old dreams of liberty and justice for all.

In developing this book, I was supported by the staff at Bobst Library at New York University and other NYU colleagues, including Dean Ellen Schall of the Wagner Graduate School of Public Service; Dean Robert Lapiner of the School of Continuing and Professional Studies (SCPS); Naomi Levine, chair and executive director of the George H. Heyman, Jr., Center for Philanthropy and Fundraising; and my graduate students at the Heyman Center of the SCPS at NYU.

Finally, I am especially grateful to IHS and OLC for constant encouragement, and to all the nuns who formed me, as well as to my mother, Vera Gaudiani, for her prayers and tireless enthusiasm, and to my family for sustaining traditions that have served me so well for so long.

To my children, Graham and Christina Burnett and Maria Burnett and Ledio Cakaj, and their children, for discussions and diversions as needed and love and affection as ever.

To David Burnett, my husband, partner, best researcher, and ultimate editor, I offer a lifetime of appreciation and love.

INTRODUCTION

Generosity Unbound is my love letter to American philanthropy, the kind of letter a loving parent might write to a successful and accomplished son or daughter. It is filled with praise and admiration, with fond memories of special moments and accomplishments. It is meant to defend and protect as only a loving parent can. But it is also a challenge to keep on striving to fulfill the potential that is as yet unrealized. As you will see, I think citizen-to-citizen generosity is among our most important national assets. It needs all the love and encouragement we can provide to help it grow and flourish. Our nation's future depends on it.

Our American system of meeting needs through freely undertaken acts of citizen-to-citizen generosity—what I am calling "generosity unbound"—is essential to who we are as a people. Our forebears created it and left it to us. It has helped millions of Americans get closer to the American Dream. It is a part of our heritage we can be genuinely proud of.

In these troubled times, we need "generosity unbound" as much or more than ever. The catastrophic recession and financial instabilities since late 2007 have left millions without jobs, home ownership, or access to higher education and health care. Endowments have lost between a quarter and a third of their value. Some foundations have actually had to close down because their funds eroded so dramatically. This suggests that needs are greater than ever and resources have been grievously reduced. To add to this serious picture, many economists believe that the repair of all this damage will evolve slowly. Even with careful investments and 5 percent spend rules, endowment recovery may take as long as job recovery. Personal engagement and courageous imagination will be more important than ever to repairing and advancing the damaged middle class and the still-suffering poorest Americans.

Of course, as our economy grows stronger and produces more jobs, American philanthropy will remain a crucial (if often underappreciated) driver of this recovery. Our American middle class has become increasingly fragile—too many of us are struggling and fearful that we won't be able to remain in it. Many others fear that they will never be able to join it at all. American-style generosity has a greater role to play than ever. Its openness to innovation and entrepreneurship can launch successful strategies to renew and expand the American middle class.[1]

Finally, we need to nurture our philanthropic tradition because it is under threat. New proposals being developed by advocacy organizations and considered by state legislatures would seriously weaken this system, perhaps substituting state or federal government regulation for the freedom of donors to give as they choose. This would be a terrible mistake, in my judgment, and I intend to demonstrate why.

On the other hand, as much as I value our American tradition of generosity, I see clearly that our system can and should improve. It should do more. It should be smarter. It should scale up what works well. And it should be more inclusive. Its critics point to its flaws, and as often as not, the critics are right. The flaws exist. Even if some of those critics are proposing solutions that would likely make things worse, we should be grateful to them for pointing to serious issues, and we should reach out to them as colleagues and fellow citizens, so that we can work together to find fresh and genuine paths forward. In this book's challenge to American philanthropy, I will suggest how this might be done.

Generosity Unbound divides into three parts. The first part is about current events—it describes the current controversy over donor freedom and the proposed new restrictions on citizen-to-citizen giving. The second part is a primer on American generosity—a brief guided tour of the origins, purposes, achievements, shortcomings, and distinctiveness of our American philanthropic tradition. And the third part is a recommendation for the future—an idea for mobilizing this philanthropic system anew to lift millions of our citizens into the broad middle class.

In sum, this book is a critical appreciation of our distinctively American approach to citizens' sharing our good fortune with others. Our philanthropic institutions grow out of values that are rooted in the ideals of our Founders. These ideals have endured to the present day. They continue to generate new ideas and inspire our history as an "improving people." The best way to love and improve our nation is to strengthen our commitment as individuals to the well-being of all our fellow citizens.

Since we will be spending some time together, I have a confession to make up front. I am an idealist. My children would say I am a hopeless idealist. I am also an optimist. My parents and the School Sisters of Notre Dame taught me to believe that it is within our power to make the world a better place. I am also a patriot, the daughter of a West Pointer, fighter pilot, and POW in Japan who taught me to love my country. I love America and the wonderful ideals of freedom and justice that our nation represents. It will not take long for you to see that each of these characteristics has influenced the views I express in *Generosity Unbound*.

You will also quickly see why I am a passionate champion of American philanthropy. Our generosity to one another makes us an exceptional nation. It reflects our idealism and our optimism about the future. I spend my life encouraging Americans to be generous to one another. I want all Americans to know how important this tradition is to our success as a nation. I want everyone to own this history and to commit to sustaining our tradition in good times and bad.

I respond negatively to ideas that threaten America's philanthropic commitments, and recent efforts by the Greenlining Institute and the National Committee for Responsive Philanthropy to promote new legislative regulation of private foundations constitute just this type of threat. Accordingly, *Generosity Unbound* offers my argument for the philanthropic sector to remain true to its own best traditions and therefore free of legislative or other incursions on its autonomy.

Yet before addressing issues of regulation, I want to focus on the bigger picture. I want to explore our tradition of generosity, and why it is important to all citizens,* not simply to people in need of help. We all need to know how the nation got to be the place it is, the place where millions of people from throughout the world have decided they want to raise their children. If citizens neglect our civic traditions of freedom, equality, and generosity, we will not understand how to keep them alive for future generations. Our kind of democracy depends on each generation's commitment to a set of ideals that need reinforcement and shared memory. *Generosity Unbound* is intended to reinforce those ideals.

I see *Generosity Unbound* as a book for everyone. Each of us is a personal beneficiary of the generosity of others. In doing generous deeds, some of us act alone and others join what

---

* By "citizen," I do not mean a legal category. Throughout this book, this word is used as a term of power defining a local participant in a democracy.

Edmund Burke called "little platoons" or what Alexis de Tocqueville called "citizen associations." Our distinctive American culture developed from citizen action. Many citizens have taken the words of the Declaration of Independence seriously. They have taken responsibility for expanding access to "life, liberty, and the pursuit of happiness" for all Americans. They have built the notion of the greater good on practical ideas like "self-interest, rightly understood." This means that "I realize that it is in my best interest to act as a good citizen towards you, because I know that you will do the same for me."* We all benefit from this idea today. No other nation in the world is built on this type of philosophical foundation.

This is a story that all Americans need to know and appreciate so we can sustain our nation in the face of international terrorism, multiple wars, intense partisanship, and the noise of a twittering blogosphere. I intend to make the case for protecting and expanding our philanthropic sector. We are all responsible to make sure it thrives throughout the twenty-first century.

Because a misguided legislative initiative prompted me to write *Generosity Unbound*, I also want to speak directly to state and federal legislators and their staffs. You have the power, and the awesome responsibility, to strengthen or weaken our national values. I want to convey the history and accomplish-

---

* Tocqueville also observed this unique American commitment in his widely cited *Democracy in America* published in 1835: "The American moralists do not profess that men ought to sacrifice themselves for their fellow creatures because it is noble to make such sacrifices; but they boldly aver that such sacrifices are as necessary to him who imposes them upon himself, as to him for whose sake they are made." Translated by Francis Bowen (Cambridge, MA: Sever and Francis, 1868), 148.

ments of our philanthropic sector in order to help you make wise judgments. I have included chapters on the basic structure of our philanthropic sector and an overview of regulation of private philanthropy as it has evolved over hundreds of years. For you, I want *Generosity Unbound* to provide an efficient source of information about American philanthropy, its deep relationship to American prosperity, and its promise as a contributor to a strong American future.

I am hopeful that legislators will see the wisdom of rejecting any initiatives that threaten to weaken our philanthropic tradition. People of color who are leaders of philanthropies are a particularly important audience, because some of these leaders represent significant numbers of lower-income citizens. Philanthropy must be a partner, not a problem, for minorities and low-income people. It is important, in this vein, to understand what foundations have done over the last 270 years to help make the words of the Declaration of Independence a reality for Americans of all races and income levels.

Despite its long history, American philanthropy is still a fragile institution. Well-meaning legislators could make the mistake of trying to force foundations to contend with additional taxes, costly legal defenses of their donors' intent, and other government incursions on their positions as private "little platoons" operating for public benefit. It is understandably tempting, in hard economic times, to impose new taxes on endowments as a way of balancing depleted municipal or state budgets. What a short-sighted idea! What a departure from our traditions! On a purely practical level, these approaches would not provide resources to those in need. They would most likely inspire foundations to give less, close down, or to move offshore. Few citizens will thank legislators for reducing the number of foundations in their communities. In addition, if newly wealthy citizens see these punitive acts toward foundations, they are likely to step back themselves from acts of voluntary generosity, including the creation of their own new foundations. So I hope, respectfully, to provide some context that will enable our elected representatives to balance the many competing interests in the legislative process, and to arrive at wise decisions concerning the protection and future of our American philanthropic tradition.

In the final chapters of *Generosity Unbound*, I want to speak to those most directly affected by recent legislative initiatives: the leaders of our private philanthropic sector. The nation very much needs civic leaders who publicly exemplify statesmanlike qualities: especially the willingness to practice "self-interest, rightly understood." Foundation leaders are positioned to do just that. Our social-profit sector has enabled some of our country's best civic work to occur in the aftermath of economic crises.* Such difficulties call for statesmanship. I believe that they also focus the hearts of Americans for special acts of generosity.

---

* The recession of 1893–96, precipitated by the failure of the Reading Railroad, caused skyrocketing unemployment and a stock market and banking collapse. The first of several general-purpose foundations was organized and chartered in the immediate aftermath of this recession. The March of Dimes began fundraising in 1937 in the midst of the grim recession of 1937–38. Eighty-nine percent of all Americans contributed, for a total of four billion dimes.

I have an idea—I want to invite foundation leaders to develop a "Declaration Initiative" to celebrate the 250th anniversary of the Declaration of Independence in 2026. The Founders wrote that "all men are created equal . . . endowed by their Creator with certain unalienable rights. . . ." In America, we are making progress, but we are not there yet. Most Americans enjoy those rights, but we need to bring everyone on board. I believe that private-citizen associations provide our best hope to get the job done. Government may be an eventual partner, but citizen associations have been doing this work since before the ink dried on our Constitution.

Can we still count on citizen initiative to fulfill the Founders' intent for our nation? Too many struggling Americans have limited longevity, little liberty, and few opportunities to pursue true happiness. But we also have creative ideas for meeting these challenges, and we are finding ways to help these ideas thrive in our social marketplace.

Our goal must be nothing less than renewing and expanding the great American middle class—creatively helping those who today are struggling, often with fading hopes, to remain a part of it, while also lifting up the many among us who are struggling, often with fading hopes, to join it. This would be the task and challenge, as I envision them, of the Declaration Initiative. Expanding the nation's middle class would create a significant asset for the future of our democracy. America still has many needs to fulfill before we could consider the Founders' intent complete. Their aspirations have been and remain our civic work. The Declaration Initiative could create a shared vision, a safe space for productive—if difficult—discussions, and the freedom for funders and implementers to test, evaluate, and scale up the very best ideas. This is exactly the kind of work the foundation sector is best able to lead.

Generosity Unbound offers my understanding of America's cultural wealth with all citizens—particularly legislators and philanthropic leaders who are citizens with unique powers and responsibilities. All of us can mobilize for the greater good of our fellow citizens and of our nation as we approach the 250th anniversary of our Declaration of Independence.

Now you can see that I am indeed a certified idealist and an irrepressible optimist. I hope that these qualities will serve me in good stead in my appointed task: to inspire my fellow citizens to continue the work that the Founding Fathers— and, as we will see, our republican mothers as well—set out for us.

Part I

Generosity Unbound:
Citizen-to-Citizen
Generosity in America

CHAPTER ONE

A Polarizing Set of Events

A polarizing event occurred in 2008 when California state assemblyman Joe Coto and state senator Mark Ridley-Thomas introduced AB 624 in the California state senate. This legislation addressed a perennial issue in the world of private philanthropy: transparency in the operation of private foundations. It would have required the largest private California foundations (those with $250 million or more in assets) to report publicly the ethnic and racial composition of their boards of trustees and of their paid staff members. In addition, they would also have been required to report annually on the number of grants and on the percentage of total grant dollars awarded to 1) organizations serving racial minority communities and 2) organizations led by ethnic minority boards and staffs. This reporting was to be done in the annual report and on the Web site of each large foundation. AB 624 did not mandate any greater representation of minorities among foundations' leadership and staffs or any changes in grant-making procedures.[1]

The foundations targeted in the legislation were clearly concerned by the prospect of government mandates affecting their operating procedures. In an eleventh-hour deal, a group of ten (ultimately nine) of the targeted private foundations, calling themselves the Foundation Coalition, offered to create a new pool of dedicated funding to support the operations and professional development of minority-led, not-for-profit groups in California. AB 624, in turn, was not acted upon in the state senate. The Foundation Coalition agreement led to some $30 million in commitments to address capacity-building in minority-led organizations in the state.[2]

This legislation was sponsored by the Greenlining Institute, a California-based policy and advocacy group critical of private foundations. The thinking behind the bill can be found in a series of reports issued by the Institute over the past five years. The first report, entitled "Fairness in Philanthropy, Part 1," was issued in 2005, followed by a 2006 report entitled "Investing in a Diverse Democracy: Foundation Giving to Minority-Led Non-Profits." The most recent report, "Funding the New Majority: Foundation Giving to Minority-Led Non-Profits," was issued in the summer of 2008. These reports offer variations on a Greenlining theme: private foundations—whether "national independent, California independent, or California community foundations," to use the

Greenlining categories—give fewer grants and a smaller percentage of their total donations to minority-led organizations than the Greenlining Institute views as appropriate.

Though the data have been sharply contested, the initial report asserted that only 3 percent of giving by these organizations had gone to minority-led not-for-profits.* The 2008 study, based on giving by the twenty-five largest national foundations, reported that 8.8 percent went to minority-led organizations. The ten largest California-based foundations gave an average of 12.3 percent of their dollars to minority-led organizations. Each of the three Greenlining reports includes recommendations aimed at the foundation community, urging more efforts to enhance the diversity of their organizations and to build the capacity and scope of minority-led organizations.

The proposed legislation and the funding agreement also piqued the interest of legislators in several additional states, including Florida, New York, and Pennsylvania. Perhaps most unsettling, it led to strident but revelatory remarks from United States Representative Xavier Becerra (D-CA), a member of the House Ways and Means Committee that determines tax policy, including policy affecting not-for-profits. Becerra dismissed philanthropy's efforts at diversity as "limited to a scattering of additional opportunities for people of color."

---

* The methodology of the Greenlining Institute (http://greenlining.org) used in preparing its 2006 report has been strongly criticized by the Statistical Assessment Service of George Mason University, a watchdog group devoted to scientific accuracy in the use of data (see http://www.stats.org). They note the lack of a random sample of foundations, the poor response rate among those queried, and the lack of a clear definition of "minority-led," among other weaknesses.

He pointed to the "underlying facts that drive the operational facts on the ground of the disproportionate giving, the disproportionate numbers internally within the nonprofit world that are skewed against people of color." He went on to assert that "most giving is local and most people give to those charities that serve them. . . . [T]hose who can give most give most to those institutions and entities they patronize. . . . We're going to have to do something to change the facts on the ground." Becerra concluded by questioning whether the "$32 billion earmark" is being used for a "public good.""*

Shortly after the California agreement, a Washington, D.C.-based advocacy group, the National Committee for Responsive Philanthropy (NCRP), issued a report entitled "Criteria for Philanthropy at Its Best." The NCRP recommendations, published in March 2009, go considerably farther than the proposed California legislation. Asserting that the needs of the "marginalized" in our society are not being met, the report advocates that private foundations devote 50 percent of their annual spending to organizations working to benefit such marginalized groups. NCRP defines marginalized people as "women, minorities, victims of violence, LBGT citizens, and the previously incarcerated." According

---

* *Wall Street Journal* editorial of Wednesday, December 24, 2008. The "$32 billion earmark" presumably refers to the total opportunity cost to the federal government of providing a tax deduction for all charitable giving ($306 billion in 2008) to all citizens and *not* to the opportunity cost of tax exemptions for donors to private foundations, which would be more on the order of $4 to $5 billion in 2008. I will discuss the specifics of the charitable deduction in detail in chapter six. For a more complete text of the congressman's remarks, see http://www.nonprofitquarterly. org/cohenreport/2008/06/03/can-diversity-make-the-cut.

to NCRP's numbers, the current percentage of annual foundation spending supporting all marginalized people is about 34 percent. Moreover, they recommend that an additional 25 percent of foundation grant-making be devoted to supporting "advocacy, organizing, and civic engagement to promote equity, opportunity, and justice in society."

The NCRP report further recommends that foundations change their usual 5 percent annual grant payout to at least 6 percent, provide at least 50 percent of grant dollars for general operating support, and provide at least 50 percent of their giving as multi-year grants. NCRP advocates that foundations spend at least 25 percent of grants on advocacy activities for the marginalized and that they maintain an engaged board of at least five people who offer a diversity of perspectives and are not compensated. The NCRP reports that 16 percent of foundations currently meet its criteria on multi-year funding and only about 7 percent meet its criteria for advocacy and organizing.

These criteria, if ever widely accepted, would certainly do more harm than good. Many experienced financial advisors would not advocate a blanket use of a 6 percent spend rule because it could undermine the long-term financial strength of foundations (the 5 percent rule is intended to protect endowments from catastrophes like the recent stock-market decline). Furthermore, the NCRP recommendations for specified expenditures, if taken literally, would drastically reduce the range and innovation of philanthropic giving in the United States. The NCRP agenda could threaten the future of charitable support for medical and scientific research, hospitals, environmental projects, colleges and universities, the arts, churches, synagogues, mosques, and many other institutions that have historically been considered charitable—unless the giving is narrowly focused on marginalized groups within those entities. Indeed, many of the greatest achievements of philanthropy—like the creation of the modern medical school or Andrew Carnegie's establishment of public libraries across the country—would not be considered "philanthropy at its best" by NCRP.

Some of the greatest losers in the scheme that NCRP advocates would be the poor and those who suffer from discrimination. These populations have a disproportionately high risk for uncontrolled diabetes, late-identified cancers, and infant and maternal mortality. They are more likely to seek need-based scholarships at institutions of higher education in order to make their mark in our society. By funding medical research and higher education, philanthropic pluralism directly benefits those whom NCRP wants to help, even if these funds are channeled to the alma maters of the wealthy. These philanthropic investments make our country a better place to work and to raise children—for all citizens. Furthermore, even a foundation that devotes all of its giving to services that open up opportunity for low-income Americans, such as the Knowledge Is Power Program (KIPP) or Teach for America, might not meet NCRP's criteria because they would not be engaging in enough "advocacy."

Finally, Congressman Becerra errs in calling the $32 billion in federal opportunity costs that incented some $300 billion in donations an "earmark." An earmark is a direct expenditure of federal tax dollars, collected involuntarily from citizens, by a member of Congress to benefit his or her constituents. An earmark thus recycles private dollars to local causes through the federal government. The charitable deduction, which creates the governmental opportunity cost, is an incentive. All Americans have access to these deductions, and they serve as a strong positive benefit to the economy nationwide. Charitable deductions encourage citizens at all income levels to share their fortunes, large or small, voluntarily. Two economists, one with liberal and one with conservative credentials, recently completed a study of the impact of foundation philanthropy on the country's economy. Among their results, they found that "each dollar that private and community foundations provided in grants and support in 2007 produced an estimated return of $8.58 in direct, economic welfare benefits."* Moreover, "the $42 billion in private and community foundation support in 2007 led to $511.9 billion in additional household income, through various multiplier effects, and additional tax revenues of $61.9 billion for the federal government, $44.7 billion for state governments, and $38.8 billion for local governments."[3]

---

* Robert J. Shapiro and Aparna Mathur, *The Social and Economic Value of Private and Community Foundations* (Washington, D.C.: Philanthropic Collaborative, 2008). Shapiro is a former U.S. Undersecretary of Commerce (1997–2001) and a policy advisor to Democratic administrations. Mathur is a research fellow at the American Enterprise Institute specializing in health care and a former World Bank advisor. The full report is available online at http://www.onestarfoundation.org. Critics have suggested that these numbers overstate the role of private foundations, but no better report exists as this book goes to print. See Leslie Lenkowsky, "In Philanthropy, It's Not Just About the Numbers," *Chronicle of Philanthropy,* January 29, 2009.

Congressman Becerra can be assured that this level of return on the charitable deduction to foundations is a productive investment in America. More importantly, the combination of personal virtue and personal freedom that drives voluntary giving has created unprecedented prosperity for great numbers of citizens over the course of our history.

The Founding Fathers would be pleased. Their confidence in the virtue of the citizenry has proven correct. I am a student of American philanthropy, and like many of my colleagues in the field, I am well aware of our centuries-long tradition of citizen generosity toward marginalized Americans. This work began with widows and orphans at the time of the American Revolution and continued through the struggles for abolition, civil rights, and those afflicted by disease, poverty, and discrimination. I am confident that many readers have volunteered to help people in these situations, as I have, throughout their professional and personal lives.

Over several months, I queried many foundation colleagues across the political spectrum about their reactions to the Greenlining and NCRP agendas. I found that they, too, were generally opposed to both. Several, like me, were sympathetic to some of the goals. More foundation transparency, more inclusive boards and staffs, and more investments in successful programs are worthy objectives—but they cannot be achieved by curtailing the freedom of those who are doing the giving. And even some funders of both Greenlining and NCRP expressed disappointment over the polarization that had occurred since the AB 624 episode. They said they had remained silent because they thought the voices of both orga- nizations were important in the field of philanthropy.*

I felt frustrated that with few exceptions (among these was Paul Brest, president of the William and Flora Hewlett Foundation) only the more "conservative" foundations were speaking out against something that foundations across the political spectrum thought ill-advised. Thus, I accepted an offer to develop and publish a book on the subject. I believe that we Americans are not generous because we are rich; we are rich because of our generosity to one another. I be- lieve that the Founding Fathers intended citizen generosity to be a fundamental virtue in our democracy. Such virtues cannot be legislated into existence. Given my belief in the importance of private foundations and my concern for the nation's least advantaged citizens, I want to demonstrate why the Greenlining/NCRP approach is wrong and to offer a better way forward. Let me begin by sharing the rest of my disagreements with the NCRP approach.

First, the NCRP definition of "marginalized citizens" trivializes the term by expanding the definition. Adding the U.S. population percentages of women (51), blacks (13), gays and lesbians (between 2 to 10 percent), and the aged (13 per- cent over 65), NCRP's "marginalized" population consists of well over 60 percent of the U.S. population.[4] The rest of the minority population and the formerly incarcerated might take the number above 70 percent. It is simply false that all people

---

* One of NCRP's funders actually did cancel its membership in the commit- tee and asked the organization to return its latest ($10,000) grant.

in these categories experience marginalization. In most cases, marginalization occurs when two or more categories overlap with financial insecurity. America absolutely has marginalized people, but not as NCRP defines them.

Secondly, we should all have little confidence in recommendations that direct significantly more funds to the needs of the poor without any goals for what difference these funds should achieve in people's lives over time. NCRP offers no description of the specific transformations that they intend the approximately $22 billion a year to create. How will the world be improved through these new investments? This approach to philanthropy flies in the face of recent efforts to achieve more effective philanthropy through a new set of tools that several organizations have been developing to measure progress per dollar spent in the field.*

If they had been asked, I am confident that many diverse colleagues in the field would have told NCRP that its definition of "Criteria for Philanthropy at Its Best" would do more harm than good. Such a narrow approach threatens American philanthropic pluralism and guarantees rejection—even among the very large number of people in the field who agree with both NCRP and Greenlining that too many Americans lack ready access to life, liberty, and the pursuit of happiness.

---

* The Center for Effective Philanthropy (CEP) offers a "Grantee Perception Report," an "Applicant Perception Report," and a "Staff Perception Report," assuring total anonymity for those reporting. Results are sent to the trustees and/or executives of the foundation requesting the report on their work. Numerous new books and articles have appeared that offer approaches to guide funders to more effective grant making.

We must together figure out the best way to address this challenge in the philanthropic sector. But in so doing, we should take a page from the medical profession: *Primum, non nocere*—"Above all, do no harm."

I also expected to see some acknowledgment of the successes foundations have had in moving marginalized groups toward the standard of living of the nation's middle class. The statistics offered by both groups imply, however—and in a heavy-handed way—a failure of the foundation sector. Yet there are impressive data that show success, such as the drop in infant mortality rates achieved by the Nurse-Family Partnership for low-income mothers, a program funded by the Edna McConnell Clark Foundation. Or they could have included the breakthroughs achieved by the Robert Wood Johnson Foundation in training community health assistants (promotoras), whose work has reduced blindness and amputations in diabetics by 50 percent. Or they might have mentioned the fact that the Philanthropy Roundtable currently devotes about a third of its resources to programs and publications on philanthropic strategies for expanding opportunity for low-income Americans. In addition, the Roundtable's major recent initiative, tentatively called "Helping People to Help Themselves," emphasizes philanthropic strategies for boosting business formation and growth, asset ownership, and job placement and promotion among needy populations. This effort also supports opportunities to participate in such community-based groups as scouting, youth sports, and mentoring. It sponsors groups to strengthen marriages and families, helping low-income families advance toward the security and well-being that many middle-income Americans currently enjoy. The Greenlining and NCRP reports simply do not offer a platform on which change for the greater good can be built.

While a number of specific elements in the Greenlining and NCRP reports were disappointing, worrisome, or missing, there is also a larger philosophical issue. The effort to use legislation to impose their recommendations is surely wrong-headed. It is possibly legally untenable as well. While I concur that a diverse board, staff, and grant-making profile would enrich the work of most foundations, private foundations are . . . private entities. Each has the right and obligation to decide these matters for itself. I deeply respect our nation's historic commitment to the rule of law and the distinctions between private and public, starting with illegal search and seizure laws. The less powerful are more vulnerable to suppression of privacy rights than other citizens. Individual freedoms and privacy rights are critically important to all citizens across the income spectrum, and the philanthropic world should surely not be a sole exemption.

For instance, private hospitals are not forced to offer procedures that would interfere with the principles of the institution. A foundation focused on women's needs may decide to have a board composed only of women. A foundation working for a specific religious community may elect to compose its board solely of members of that faith community. Likewise, family foundations sometimes opt for a board of family members only. My own experience affirms the significant value of diverse views in virtually all leadership structures, but these private choices ultimately yield a kind of diversity, a pluralism that is a great strength of our democracy.

Naomi Schaefer Riley's recent paper on this issue is entitled "American Philanthropic Diversity: What It Means, Why It Matters."[5] Riley points out that if each foundation board were required to mirror some larger "diversity," such as the U.S. population or a certain proportion of "marginalized" citizens, all boards would look the same. Riley suggests that diversity is served in our country by having many different foundations developing idiosyncratic profiles for their boards and developing a widely diverse universe of foundation trustees, without having enforced sameness by diversifying each board individually.

I support intelligent efforts to inform trustees of the benefits of inclusivity. Wise, appropriate, and free diversity decisions would likely enable trustees to operate their foundations even more effectively.[*] But fundamentally, it is trustee

---

[*] McKinsey & Company produced a 2007 study that confirms that a diverse workforce increases a company's competitiveness by providing greater independence of opinions and initiatives. Many studies offer ways for organizations to measure the impact of diversity in their productivity. Among these are Edward E. Hubbard, *The Diversity Scorecard: Evaluating the Impact of Diversity on Organizational Performance* (Oxford: Elsevier, 2004) and Margaret S. Stockdale and Faye J. Crosby, eds., *The Psychology and Management of Workplace Diversity* (Malden, MA: Blackwell Publishing, 2004). For the record, diversity is generally defined as acknowledging, understanding, accepting, valuing, and celebrating differences among people with respect to age, class, ethnicity, gender, physical and mental ability, race, sexual orientation, spiritual practice, and public-assistance status. See Katharine Esty, Richard Griffin, and Marcie Schorr Hirsh, *Workplace Diversity: A Manager's Guide to Solving Problems and Turning Diversity into a Competitive Advantage* (Holbrook, MA: Adams Media Corporation, 1995).

integrity and wisdom that should guide this work, not formulas or threats.* AB 624 created both.

In resorting to legislative interventions to advance its case, Greenlining showed little confidence in the good will of the foundation sector. To add to the disruption in the sector, California AB 624 was followed quickly by NCRP's threats of additional legislation. In reading both the published introduction to "Criteria for Philanthropy at Its Best" and a pre-publication version, Paul Brest noticed that

> while NCRP disclaims any "call for regulatory action," the introduction to . . . the version that NCRP sent around for pre-publication endorsements was more direct: "Policymakers may find the criteria valuable when considering regulations or legislation that affect institutional grant makers." For anyone who has experienced the Greenlining Institute's efforts to legislate social justice philanthropy in California and watched its efforts in other states, this lets the cat out of the bag. NCRP

---

* Diversity in Philanthropy is a "multi-year, multi-million dollar effort . . . driven initially by five key anchor institutions or networks: the Council on Foundations, the Foundation Center, various regional associations of grant makers, a coalition of diversity-focused funds represented by Rockefeller Philanthropy Advisors, and leading members of the Joint Affinity Groups." For a full presentation, see http://www.diversityinphilanthropy.com/news/principles-practices. In 2009, the council released its report entitled "Career Pathways to Philanthropic Leadership." The Foundation Center has a resource entitled "Diversity in Philanthropy: A Comprehensive Bibliography of Resources Related to Diversity Within the Philanthropic and Nonprofit Sectors." This work is available for download at http://foundationcenter.org/getstarted/topical/diversity.html.

has just concealed Greenlining's fist in a velveteen glove.[6]

Finally, the Greenlining/NCRP legislative initiative forced state and federal legislators to stand with them or against them before any appeal was made to the philanthropic sector itself. These tactics have further alienated many foundation leaders. Some of them began to take public positions defending their work and the field against both Greenlining and NCRP. Imagine the concern when Greenlining's new head, Orson Aguilar, explained on the organization's Web site how he had been working to export the idea of legislating foundation spending across the nation:

> Other states are responding as well. Community leaders in Florida, New York, and New Jersey are urging their lawmakers to introduce similar legislation, and lawmakers in Pennsylvania are currently conducting background research to determine if a similar bill would be appropriate for their state. We hope these efforts across the country will encourage the U.S. Congress to take the next step and make this a national public policy issue.[7]

In addition to encouraging more legal incursions into the field of private philanthropy, the NCRP process included trademarking the term "Philanthropy at Its Best." This move invited the charge of arrogance. Paul Brest expressed this point in the first of his four articles criticizing the NCRP report. Brest writes: "By trademarking the unremarkable phrase 'Philanthropy at Its Best,' the organization apparently aspires to create a philanthropic version of the *Good Housekeeping* Seal of Approval."[8] Brest was widely quoted calling NCRP's report "breathtakingly arrogant." Two associations of grant makers, the Council on Foundations and the Philanthropy Roundtable, also raised objections to the NCRP's standards. Surprised by the vigorous opposition, Aaron Dorfman, NCRP executive director, added what he dubbed a "myth-busting page" to the organization's Web site in an effort to rebut the criticism.

Had either Greenlining or NCRP acted more inclusively in seeking guidance from colleagues in the field, I feel sure they could have advanced their important case for the people who need philanthropy's attention without alienating their supporters. I understand that Greenlining attempted to engage some members of the field and that it instigated the legislation when these overtures were ignored. Aguilar complains about foundations' reactions to the Greenlining efforts:

> the foundation community has disputed these studies, attacking them on the grounds of what they call poor methodology and unreliable data. At Greenlining, we requested meetings with foundations on numerous occasions to determine what the best methodology would be for tracking grants to communities of color, but we didn't receive a response. And on many occasions, we requested diversity

data from foundations, only to be turned away or completed ignored.[9]

After this admittedly disappointing experience, Greenlining staff might have sought the advice of any of the academic centers on philanthropy. It is hard to believe they would have been rebuffed. Or if they had addressed the trustees of the Council on Foundations, the Philanthropy Roundtable, and the Association of Small Foundations (to name just one possible line-up) to seek collegial advice on how their efforts could enhance the foundation field, I cannot believe they would have been ignored. If the collaboration had happened, I dare say that a totally different use of many people's time and money would have developed over the past two years. We might even be much farther along in pursuit of transparency and more inclusive leadership in philanthropy than the field demonstrates today.

Greenlining and NCRP have notable, experienced board members and advisors, including Pablo Eisenberg, whom many consider among the most influential and outspoken leaders in the field of philanthropy. So another possibility is that the content, process, and even the timing of the Greenlining and NCRP reports were planned to occur as they did and have the effect they did. It is difficult to understand, however, what such a strategy might achieve over the long run. The approach has alienated many colleagues from each other and hardened positions that operate more productively when working relationships are genuinely collaborative.

For instance, projects engaging more liberally oriented foundations with more conservative ones are underway in a number of cities. Politically diverse foundations are sharing the effort to address the educational challenges that poor children face. Foundations with specific expertise are working together to advance school readiness and success throughout the educational system, one of the surest pathways to middle-class security. The subtle working relationships of these foundations deserve encouragement, not provocative reminders of their differences, especially not in our over-polarized society.

Both Greenlining and NCRP have chosen to speak from isolated, negative positions. The field of social enterprise, including foundations and advocates, deserves broad-based leadership that reflects an appreciation of philanthropy's history even as it challenges all of us to do better. Philanthropy is a fast-changing, opportunistic field where the youngest members are part of a can-do generation. They are not fighting the battles of the 1960s over again. They have arrived at adulthood having done more volunteer work in high school and college than any other generation in the nation's history. They are ready to raise standards so that people in low-income conditions have access to opportunities to join the American mainstream. Many embrace strong commitments to the greatest amount of good for the largest number of citizens. Both Greenlining and NCRP missed a great opportunity to lead with optimism and appreciation.

I have argued that AB 624 constitutes a threat to private philanthropy. Sadly, threats often provoke counter-threats.

Capital is mobile. As I have pursued my research, a number of foundation leaders quietly warned that they were prepared to spend down their endowments and close their foundations if their time and money was going to be spent litigating the right to operate as private entities. Others said they had already opened preliminary inquiries on options to move their foundations offshore in order to preserve their freedom to operate as they choose. It seems strange for two groups dependent on philanthropy to launch strategies based so plainly on "biting the (private) hand that feeds." It seems even stranger, at a time when confidence in government is at an all-time low, to propose extending government regulation of the foundation sector. I believe, however, that both sectors are capable of more productive work. I intend to suggest how American history and our history of philanthropy can illuminate some promising directions for all of us and perhaps even mend some fences.

Having pointed out my concerns, let me make clear that I understand some of the factors that may have spurred NCRP and Greenlining into action. Over the past twenty-five years, private-foundation philanthropy has become increasingly visible and politically attractive. The "rock star" status of successful financiers and technology moguls has shined a spotlight on their charitable contributions, which have reached billions of dollars. From Ted Turner, T. Boone Pickens, Bill Cosby, and Richard Branson in the 1980s, to Michael Dell, Oprah Winfrey, Pierre Omidyar, and Michael Bloomberg since then, celebrity giving is a new game to watch. Stars like George Clooney and Angelina Jolie have made both donating and volunteering a new celebrity sport. Cause marketing is no longer a fad. It is a necessity for selling everything from luxury goods to breakfast cereal.

We have entered a new golden age of large-scale giving by successful capitalists. The sheer size of the Bill and Melinda Gates Foundation, with $30-odd billion in assets, is hard to miss. Warren Buffett's pledge of an additional $1.5 billion per year in spendable funds to Gates only adds to the magnitude of the enterprise. Although giving by "average" citizens still constitutes by far the largest component of voluntary giving in the U.S. (about 80 percent of 2009's $300 billion, if bequests are included), foundations represent an ever more prominent feature of the national landscape financially and psychologically.

Greater visibility and growing assets have also increased public and governmental interest in, and even suspicion of, the world of foundations, as was the case a century ago following the Gilded Age. Now, as then, citizens are sensitive to very great disparities in income distribution, exaggerated by the publicity surrounding Wall Street's salaries and bonuses handed out in the midst of the Great Recession. Under such circumstances, trust in private foundations is often inversely related to the size of the fortunes involved. Of course, periodic scandals involving self-dealing by trustees and other abuses, even though very rare both then and now, further erode public confidence and invite governmental scrutiny.

Given the startling deterioration of many municipal and state governments as the economic crisis of late 2007 deepened, the funds stored in foundation endowments undoubtedly looked very appealing as assets that could be made available to fill burgeoning budget holes. They may look even more appealing today, as government indebtedness increases and some states have begun to tax haircuts and popcorn at the movies to try to replace funds lost from reduced income and real estate taxes.

Having acknowledged these realities, I repeat that there are great dangers in treating foundation assets as a piggybank. Foundation endowments are private property held for the public benefit according to the donor's intent. Tax deductions for charitable donations were established to provide an incentive to sustain our tradition of citizen generosity. Deductions for many additional expenditures are offered as well. Deductible contributions do not, however, make foundation endowments any more public than are the homes of citizens who have elected to deduct their mortgage-interest payments from their taxes. As we will see in chapter four, any such challenge would undoubtedly be argued in court and probably go to the Supreme Court. The time and money involved deserves to go to public benefit, not to polarizing litigation.

American citizens are the most generous people on earth. This generosity feeds mutuality and engenders patriotism. These values were important to Ben Franklin and Thomas Jefferson and they are just as important today. Those of us in the philanthropic sector have a leadership opportunity to strengthen these values. We need to share our knowledge of our nation's history and the role that philanthropy has played in the creation of our national prosperity under the rule of law. We need our legislators and public servants to understand this contribution and the cultural importance of the tradition of generosity. In a time of fragmentation and politicization of public discourse, our country needs collaborative civic leadership from private foundations. This work can gradually remind the nation of our Founders' intent as expressed in the Declaration of Independence—our national mission statement that they left for us to complete. This work can also reassert America's most important power, her moral leadership.

Japanese Americans suffered terribly with the forced evacuation, and a guy like me, fortunate enough to have succeeded in business, should help keep the memories alive.

–George Aratani,
founder of Mikasa and Kenwood, Inc.,
upon funding a chair in Japanese Internment
Studies at UCLA (among his $10 million
in philanthropic gifts)

CHAPTER TWO

Generosity Drives the American Economy

America's culture of philanthropy has defined both our society and our economy. The idea of American exceptionalism has a rich history of supporters and detractors, but our philanthropy alone makes the case for our exceptionalism. Most modern nations share a tradition of government by monarchy. Citizens expect government to attend to the needs of the citizenry, just as an enlightened monarch was expected to attend to the needs of his or her subjects. Taxes flow to the central government and are redistributed to the people through a centralized and, ideally, rational bureaucracy. The American model for the support of good causes is decentralized, unmanaged, and pluralistic. These values define our philanthropic tradition. On this basis alone, we are exceptional—if not always in the sense of "better," certainly in the sense of "different."

We are the most generous people on earth. Generosity is our most widely held value. Eighty-nine percent of Americans make a charitable donation each year. Giving constitutes our most widely shared community activity, far beyond eating fast food, watching the Super Bowl, or voting.

Generosity is in our blood as Americans, no matter when or how our ancestors got to these shores. Generosity is a value shared by the well-to-do and the not-so-well-to-do. It is shared across races and ethnic origins. Our solidarity as donors makes us all feel responsible for the well-being of our fellow Americans and of our nation.*

Generous Americans give to causes that compel our attention regardless of our personal connections. Of course, we give to support causes that we are personally connected to: our religious communities, our schools, and to help people who share the same problems or diseases that we have confronted. But we also give to create opportunities for others to whom we have no direct connection. Newcomers naturally favor their own families and communities, but they quickly see that this is not the only way that Americans give. Americans from Elizabeth Ann Seton and Lillian Wald to Julius Rosenwald, Andrew Carnegie, Kenneth Langone, Marie Lam,

---

* This idea is reflected in the robust commitment of minorities to the giving tradition. The Community Investment Network is one of many programs devoted to extending the efforts of black philanthropists (http://www.thecommunityinvestment. org). The First Nations Development Institute leads Native-American philanthropic efforts (http://www.firstnations.org), and there are many leadership efforts in Hispanic philanthropy, including Hispanics in Philanthropy (http://www.hiponline. org). Asian Americans and Pacific Islanders have a philanthropy organization as well (http://aapip.org).

and Eugene Lang came from immigrant families and became remarkable philanthropists: Catholics, Protestants, and Jews, Germans, Scots, Italians, Chinese, and Hungarians giving across boundaries to benefit the greater good. So many other names could be listed with these.

Few Americans ask where this generosity came from. Why has it continued? Will it remain a part of American culture? The answers to these questions create a source of honest pride in our history and our ancestors—pride we often do not get a chance to celebrate. America's tradition of citizen-to-citizen generosity, what I am calling "generosity unbound," comes from a long-standing connection between personal wealth and the common good. I want to tell the story of how these connections were built, and I think it is easier to care about the history when we know the people involved. Individuals make the biggest difference when they put their values into action. So let me introduce George Peabody.

Peabody (1795–1869) was a legendary wealth-builder. He also established the country's earliest philanthropic institution. He set a standard that influenced generations to come. First, he made gifts as investments in the present on behalf of the future. Second, he made this "donor intent" clear in his various gifts. Third, he encouraged his wealthy business associates to follow in his footsteps.

Peabody grew up in a poor Massachusetts household of eleven children with strong Puritan grounding. His father made a meager living by subsistence farming and working in casual leather in Massachusetts. George had to leave school early to support his mother and siblings. He worked as a laborer and then ran a general store in his hometown before a disastrous fire induced him to move south with his uncle to open a general store in Washington, D.C. When his military service in the War of 1812 ended, he joined a partnership with Elisha Riggs in Georgetown. He spent years traveling in the United States and England buying and selling dry goods.

Substantial wealth-building began in America after the War of 1812. The agricultural economy slowly gave way to the industrial economy that would advance through the nineteenth century. Production moved gradually from work done by hand and at home to work done by machine and at a factory or mine. An industrial revolution laid railroads, set steamship routes, and put machines in farmers' hands—and the country began to change. These technologies required large sums of money to develop before they began to pay off, so investors were needed who could supply funds. These investors in stocks or bonds waited patiently for the businesses to pay them back. Merchant banks and both domestic and international finance played a vital role in the transformation of America from an agricultural to an industrial society.

Peabody moved to London, where he opened his own financial firm in 1843. He dealt with mercantile traders and also bought and sold bonds. He was especially committed to selling American bonds in Europe to help finance capital-intensive projects like the canals and railroads that enabled our country's westward expansion. As an investment banker, he achieved the financing for the laying of the first transatlantic cable. His

London business was a partnership with Junius S. Morgan, and Peabody helped train Junius's son, J. P., in international banking. The younger Morgan began his career as a New York representative of George Peabody & Co.

Peabody saw how investments of patient capital made striking progress possible. America's railroads and other capital-intensive industries grew. Brokerage firms developed and securities were sold enabling investors in England and America to advance progress and also to amass fortunes. The paths were set for the Gilded Age. Peabody was also blazing another trail, the one to the golden age of major philanthropic institutions.

Peabody treated his wealth as the good steward did in the Bible.* He was deeply committed to the betterment of all mankind. This belief was best served, he concluded, by investments in education and opportunities for learning that he had not found in his own youth. The Peabody institutes and museums were his effort to make self-improvement available to all people. He invested in scientific research in fields like archaeology and anthropology. In England, he invested in housing for the urban working poor.

In 1852, on the one hundredth anniversary of the founding of his native town of Danvers, Massachusetts, Peabody—who was still in England—sent a letter to be read at the town celebration. In part it said: "In acknowledgement of

---

* Acts 20:35. The biblical principal of stewardship teaches that what I have is not mine alone to use however I wish. It is instead a gift from God to be used wisely and carefully in accord with God's love of the world.

the payment of that debt by the generation which preceded me in my native town of Danvers, and to aid in its prompt future discharge, I give to the inhabitants of that town the sum of TWENTY THOUSAND DOLLARS, for the promotion of knowledge and morality among them."[1]

The funds were invested in a town lyceum, where the eight-hundred-seat auditorium hosted lectures, concerts, theatre performances, and other learning opportunities for the citizenry. Peabody wisely left funds for the building's upkeep and for annual cash prizes to the town's most gifted students. He also gave his hometown its motto: "Education—a debt due from the present to future generations."

Peabody's work brought him into contact with many entrepreneurs: Johns Hopkins, John Goodyear, and Cornelius Vanderbilt, among others. They admired his financial acumen and his great philanthropy. Peabody's arguments in favor of education as a national solidifying force after the Civil War convinced Vanderbilt to endow Vanderbilt University in Nashville, Tennessee. Paul Tulane was directly influenced by Peabody to found Tulane University in New Orleans, and Anthony Drexel was moved to found Drexel University in Philadelphia.[2] Another of Peabody's colleagues, Johns Hopkins, was persuaded to endow the nation's first graduate university in Baltimore.

Peabody believed that an educated citizenry transcended political partisanship. He funded the Peabody Institute of Baltimore and then engaged his hand-picked trustees in a cooperative venture pursuing social advancement through education. The year 1857 included a financial panic and the rumblings of civil war, but Peabody kept his wealthy colleagues committed to the Institute even when they found themselves in financial uncertainty and on opposite sides of the slavery issue. The Institute provided a library, programs of lectures, an academy of music, a gallery of art, and prizes to encourage private- and public-school children to excel in their studies. Peabody himself offered the following guidance: an "injunction against the Institute's ever being used for the nurture of Sectarian theology, or political dissension." The Institute was to "show itself, in every emergency, the firm defender of our 'Glorious Union.'"[3]

Peabody returned to Danvers from London in 1868, when the town was renamed for him. He found a thriving community that, he was proud to discover, was spending five times more dollars on public elementary education than had been spent when he was a boy. In his speech to the community, he underlined the importance of education. "To be truly great," he said, "it is not necessary to gain wealth or importance. Every boy may become a great man in whatever sphere Providence places him in. Truth and integrity, unsullied by unworthy acts, constitutes greatness."[4]

Peabody invested in additional institutes at Harvard and Yale, and in Baltimore and Danvers, but his largest philanthropic initiative was funding education in the South through the Peabody Education Fund, which he established at the end of the Civil War. In the founding letter, dated 1867, Peabody wrote that "the moral and intellectual development [of the

United States] should keep pace with her material growth. . . . [T]he impoverished people of the South cannot, without aid, advance themselves in knowledge and power."[5]

Scarcely two years after Appomattox, and for the first time since the end of the Civil War, former governors from northern and southern states stood together at the ceremony deeding George Peabody's multimillion-dollar gift. Peabody stood with General Ulysses Grant and a local bishop as the deed of the gift was read. It was praised as "the first guarantee of a reunited Country and of perpetual Union."

Peabody's fund was a milestone in American philanthropy. As his biographer notes:

> The PEF, governed by a board of trustees from both North and South, was the first multimillion dollar foundation in the United States that exercised a positive attitude toward solving social ills. It was this nation's first educational foundation without religious conditions, the first whose influence was national, the first to provide for modification as conditions changed, and the first to set a pattern of selecting trustees from the professions and business.[6]

No one could have anticipated the power of this precedent-setting gift. It educated thousands, and it also inspired other philanthropists. It set expectations for good governance that still hold today. John Slater, a Connecticut textile magnate, donated $1 million to advance the "uplifting of the lately emancipated population of the Southern States" in 1882. Slater so admired Peabody that he decided to advance his goal by focusing his funds on the education of African-American children. Anna T. Jeanes, a Philadelphia Quaker, deeded $1 million to the education of southern African-American children in 1905. Modeled after the great work of Virginia Cabell Randolph, a black teacher in the Richmond area, Jeanes Fund teachers visited students in their homes and helped to improve health and sanitation as well as to advance education. The Slater and Jeans funds were combined with others in 1937 to create the Southern Education Fund, which continues to this day. Peabody's trustees remained true to his intent that his fund be dissolved after thirty years. The remaining assets were contributed to the Peabody Normal School that they had established. Today, the Peabody College for Teachers is part of Vanderbilt University.

George Peabody defines the values that have become emblematic of Americans who create foundations. He exemplifies our philanthropic tradition of generosity unbound. He believed in hard work and the building of personal wealth. But he saw himself as a trustee of this wealth, and thus he invested in others so the future would be better—for them and for the nation. He sought a public impact from his wealth, rather than a purely private benefit. He supported his own community and the parts of his nation that were in most need of new assets in order to develop for their own good and for the greater good.

Thanks to virtuous entrepreneurs like Peabody, wealth and philanthropy became more closely associated in the U.S.

than they are in any other nation. The investment model of philanthropy gives people a stake in the futures of others. It injects pride across generations, races, ethnicities, and skill sets. It is still the shaping feature of American culture in the twenty-first century.

Will this investment philanthropy continue in America? The best way to answer this question is to consider the relationship of investment philanthropy to our economy and our democracy. The best illustration of this relationship is what I call the "virtuous cycle," the engine that philanthropy has created at the core of American society. It is powerfully illustrated by the life of George Peabody.

Let me explain. American philanthropists make unregulated **investments** that create **opportunity**. A scholarship offers a worthy student an opportunity to advance his or her education. A research grant creates the opportunity for a researcher to make progress in his or her research, whether understanding disease mechanisms or climate changes. We can never have too many opportunities.

Martin Luther King, Jr., demonstrated faith in these American ideas in his famous "I Have a Dream" speech. Using a banking metaphor, he argued that black Americans had received a "bad check" from the nation, but he concluded: "we refuse to believe that there are insufficient funds in the great vaults of opportunity of this nation." He had faith in the Founders' ideals even though many of his fellow citizens had forgotten the pledge the Founders had made in their names.

Chapter Two

In the high-risk business of building a working democracy, we all need all the opportunities we can create. Our American strategy over generations has been to ensure that we educate all citizens to the absolutely highest level of their capacity. In so doing, we optimize our own chances of enjoying **prosperity**. Thus, the second step in the cycle: **Opportunity** builds **prosperity.**

Prosperity is something we know quite a bit about in America. For all our shortcomings, we have achieved a remarkable level of economic and social prosperity in the brief period of our history. We enjoy some of the highest living standards in the world. Given the vastness and diversity of our nation, we have achieved high levels of education for a large percentage of our population. We continue to make progress on the economic front. For instance, the average household income before the market crash of 1929, when translated into today's dollars, was about $16,000. In other words, the entire middle class in the 1920s was poor by today's standards. Despite some of the highest levels of income disparity in the past one hundred years, it is still true that the bottom quintile of wage earners has seen an 80 percent increase in real wages in the past fifteen years.

Prosperity, of course, is about a state of mind as much as it is about dollars and cents. One can hardly claim prosperity for a nation if a significant portion of its citizens are pessimistic about the future. But Americans are, in fact, optimistic, and those who are less well-off seem to have preserved their enthusiasm for the American Dream. Upward mobility remains a firm belief among many newcomers.[7] The spirit of entrepreneurism is alive and well, as our nation continues to create more new businesses than any other nation on earth.[8] As wrenching as the inevitable changes in our economy are for older workers and for those with less education, we have managed again and again to invent entire new industries at a remarkable pace: pharmaceuticals, biotechnology, wireless communication, Internet commerce. We have every reason to believe that the difficulties of recent years can be overcome with a continuing commitment to justice in the form of unbounded generosity.

The third step in the cycle: **Prosperity** produces **gratitude**. This next component of the virtuous cycle is among the most visible today. Virtually all of the new generation of philanthropists, following in the steps of Peabody, Sage, Carnegie, and Rockefeller, have acknowledged a desire to give back to the nation that has enabled them to amass their significant fortunes. They have recognized that the stability of the nation, its institutions and infrastructure, have enabled their enterprises to prosper. They could take no personal credit for these features of our society and they wanted to express their gratitude for finding such favorable conditions in which to develop their ideas.

There are many more participants in the tradition of American gratitude than the wealthy white men with their names on concert halls, museums, and universities. Remember that 89 percent of Americans make charitable contributions each year. In fact, the lower 40 percent of wage earners are more generous, on a percentage-of-income basis, than are the upper levels of wage earners. Most of these givers also give out of gratitude. I have the most vivid memories of my scholarship students at Connecticut College, where I served as president. When given an opportunity to thank their benefactors in person, these students regularly pledged to give back their four-year scholarships to the college as soon as they were in a position to do so.

This sense of personal responsibility in a free society is a vital asset to our nation. It keeps us focused on the needs of others, rather than on our own small worlds. We are among the few nations in the world with a holiday devoted to thanksgiving. It is certainly a most American of holidays, right up there with the national celebration of our independence. We also benefit personally from a focus on the well-being of others. A large and growing body of scientific literature documents the physical and psychological benefits to those who focus on gratitude for even the most modest blessings they enjoy.[9] So, in its turn, our gratitude induces the beginning of a new cycle. We are motivated to commit new acts of **generosity** because we are grateful for the **opportunities** from philanthropy that enabled our own **prosperity** and inspired our **gratitude**. When we make certain to acknowledge that we, too, are beneficiaries of the generosity of our fellow citizens, we ensure our role in sustaining the virtuous cycle. After all, most of us did not get polio; many of us have a pension that is invested in diversified investments; many of us have used the 911 system in an emergency and taken an antibiotic.

These are all gifts from philanthropists to the rest of us! So even if you never received a scholarship or never sought help at a free medical clinic, you and I are still recipients of philanthropy from our fellow citizens. Therefore, we owe back!

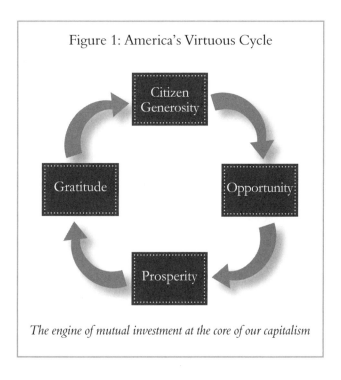

Figure 1: America's Virtuous Cycle

Citizen Generosity

Opportunity

Prosperity

Gratitude

The engine of mutual investment at the core of our capitalism

Americans have a long list of gifts to be thankful for. If you or your children need an example or two to remember why you have reason to be grateful to others for their generosity to you, read on.

How Philanthropy Has Strengthened
Our Economy and Our Democracy

American-style philanthropy creates a balance between capitalism and democracy. It strengthens both. It feeds optimism and innovation. It enables everyone to see the importance of fairness. It reminds us of the Founders' expectations that we each take personal responsibility for "life, liberty, and the pursuit of happiness" for our fellow citizens. It is important to recall the conclusion of the Declaration of Independence: "And for the support of this Declaration, with a firm reliance on the protection of Divine Providence, we mutually pledge to each other our Lives, our Fortunes, and our sacred Honor."

Capitalism is wealth producing and wealth concentrating. A market economy fosters tough competition and potentially winner-take-all outcomes. It encourages optimization of the individual's assets. It is demanding, impatient, imaginative, and entrepreneurial. It thrives on freedom and light bureaucracy. It is risk tolerant, but also self-focused. Enterprises must continue to grow or they risk being overtaken by competitors and simply withering away. But there is little evidence that democracy can thrive when income distributions reach very high levels of inequality.

Therefore, free-market capitalism needs a wise governor on its engine, and philanthropy provides such a mechanism. It prevents capitalism from "overheating" and burning itself up. Karl Marx theorized at the beginning of the industrial revolution that capitalists would eventually own all the means of production. Workers would have little choice but to rise up and overthrow the capitalists and confiscate their wealth. Marx's prediction had its own internal logic. He did not, however, imagine the combination of virtue and enterprise found in men such as Peabody, Slater, and many others whom we will meet in subsequent chapters. They applied a control mechanism to their engine of wealth-building. That mechanism is personal philanthropy. Philanthropy has made our capital-market system work as well as it has because it emphasizes fair play and self-discipline. When our system has failed us, it has usually been because greed shoved generosity out of its way. The children of wealth may end up with fewer material resources if their parents choose to start a foundation. They end up with more spiritual resources when their parents have taught them generosity. Generosity in turn launches potential new capitalists from poorer families. The nation grows as this new energy competes with legacy wealth, advancing our economy and our democracy.

Capitalism, on the other hand, is an excellent teacher for those committed to building our civil society. We have a robust tradition of social entrepreneurship that is heavily indebted to the best features of capitalism: a clear vision, disciplined strategy, capital raising, and scalability, plus those essential intangibles—optimism and determination. In America, social entrepreneurship has been part of our history since the beginning. Eugene Lang offers one example of social entrepreneurship. When he talked to a sixth-grade class in his old grammar school, he was struck with an idea. Why not offer his own funds to pay for college for any of them who could graduate from high school? Through optimism and determination and trial and error, he developed a plan for these youngsters to succeed. Over time, his work has inspired dozens of additional idealistic, optimistic social entrepreneurs to duplicate his idea.* Today, thousands of low-income children have persevered through grammar and high school and received funded college educations thanks to these efforts. Lang's I Have a Dream Foundation has all the traits of a fine new entry into the business world in a capital-market system: innovative problem-solving, focus, a willingness to keep working to improve the product and process, and scalability. Wendy Kopp's Teach for America provides another example. From a first group of two hundred young recruits in 1989, Teach for America has scaled up its teacher corps to 7,300 members who taught more than 450,000 students in our country's neediest communities in 2009. These are illustrations of how foundations make pervasive and transformational change in our democracy.

Philanthropy feeds both democratic values and our market economy by investments that foster upward mobility. It creates jobs and contributes to raising our standard of living. Philanthropy acknowledges that life is not automatically fair and engages wealth in addressing unfairness. Some people are born on third base while others have never even

---

* One such entrepreneur of special note in our current environment is Fred Clark, a successful Mexican-American businessman whose foundation provides scholarships for low-income Mexican-American kids in California. Only in America . . .

held a bat before the game begins. This latter group will need a break to compete, but they might turn out to be great assets to the team. Philanthropy offers such breaks. This has been our country's experience. Americans love fairness. Much of philanthropy's work has been about evening up the competition.

Philanthropy advanced education and job training for immigrants and minorities through settlement houses, child-labor laws, support to the arts and music, and health (research dedicated to defeating polio, cancer, heart disease, and for community health care). The nation's first symphony orchestras were filled by musicians who held their first violins, cellos, or saxophones in the basements of settlement houses in after-school programs. These investments in well-being came from foundations. They advanced American society and the economy in powerful ways. They are still doing so.

Philanthropy is American capitalism's trust builder and hope builder. It doesn't require that citizens be perfect. It does require us to recognize the importance of "self-interest, rightly understood." I see that it is in my best interest to watch out for your well-being and treat you with honesty and respect—because I see that this will inspire you to treat me in the same way. This reciprocity creates a strong society built on mutuality, safer for everyone's children and grandchildren. It is the reason that America remains relatively free of cynicism and bitter distrust. "Self-interest, rightly understood" is the idea that enables philanthropy to link market capitalism and democracy.

Chapter Two

Philanthropy Invests in Human, Physical, and Intellectual Capital

Philanthropy shapes our society and drives our economy through investments in human, physical, and intellectual capital. Human capital investments are donations to develop fellow citizens. Physical capital investments fund buildings, parks, and conservation. Intellectual capital investments fund new ideas in social change, technology, medicine, the arts, and other fields.

Most people have not thought about how funders transform the economy and the society around them, but each of these categories includes dramatic changes that affect the larger population. For instance, donations to programs that enhance early-childhood education or high school graduation rates—or to need-based college scholarships—are all investments in human capital. The nation prospers when such individuals, their families, and their communities benefit from this type of philanthropy. How many ordinary and amazing individuals have arrived where they are because they were "brought to you by (fill in the donor's name)."

I think that everyone who has gotten a private scholarship should wear such a name tag during Thanksgiving week. Your surgeon, your child's pediatrician or teacher, the neighborhood pharmacist, your broker, or your pastor, rabbi, or imam probably all received private financial aid at some point in their preparation to provide for you. We would all learn a lot about why our country works so well by measuring the value of the human assets that our citizen-to-citizen generosity has built for the nation.

John Rogers, founder and CEO of Ariel Investments, established his foundation to help schoolchildren in his native Chicago attend college. He was inspired by Gene Lang's "dreamers." But Rogers had a different idea. He launched the Ariel Community Academy, a charter school with a unique curriculum in one of the poorest neighborhoods of the city. In addition to studying "reading and writing and 'rithmetic," students become investment managers—with real money! By the time they reach grades seven and eight, students form a committee of peers to manage the $20,000 school fund. Upon graduation, the class awards half of their earnings to the school in the form of a class gift and divides up the other half among themselves, either as cash or for investment in their own 529 accounts (matched by the foundation if they make this choice). No surprise, the students' performance on standardized tests is among the best in the city, despite the poverty of their neighborhood. The Gates Foundation is likewise a major supporter of math, science, and engineering education for minority kids, with Bill Gates noting his lack of confidence in the federal government to address this issue creatively.

Clare Boothe Luce left her entire bequest to the support of girls and women for careers in math, the physical sciences, and engineering. The Luce Foundation has stewarded Mrs. Luce's gift, which has provided 1,550 awardees with $120 million over the past several decades.* Oprah Winfrey continued

---

* Full disclosure: I am a member of the selection committee of the Clare Boothe Luce Fund, along with Midge Decter, Edwin J. Feulner, James Piereson, David V. Ragone, and Cynthia M. Friend. The fund is part of the Henry Luce Foundation, where I also serve as a trustee.

this important work with her Angel Network Foundation that attracted some 80,000 donors to support education for girls during its years of operation. Remarkable entrepreneur that she is, Oprah has leveraged her generosity just as George Peabody did. In Oprah's case, she has used her media expertise to engage thousands of givers in her "Big Give" programs. Oprah does it and teaches others to do it.

But philanthropic human capital investments go well beyond young people. Foundations support programs to permit people over age twenty-five to receive counseling and scholarships to start college as adults. Men and women in prison have access to foundation support in many states to advance their formal education during incarceration, thus improving lives and reducing recidivism. Foundations support programs to address the special needs of groups whose life development may have been thwarted for various reasons. Special Olympics is one great example among many. Autism Speaks is another. Philanthropy, especially foundation giving, is the haven for second (and third) chances for our fellow citizens all over America.

"Physical capital" describes another major category of American philanthropic investment. Gardens, parks, and playgrounds all over the country have come from the gifts of generous donors for centuries. How many libraries, hospitals, colleges, schools, museums, recreational areas, theatres, shelters, and science institutes in your own town or city are the gifts of generous fellow citizens? What would a Google map of your town look like if they all vanished tonight? "Very, very different" is the likely answer.

These gifts keep on giving. They provide opportunities and services that improve the quality of life and attract populations to the locales in which they are located. They provide jobs for the people who work in them. They improve the real estate values surrounding them. They provide business opportunities for nearby small businesses. These facilities attract people. Tens of millions visit campuses, libraries, museums, parks, and hospitals each year. They use local transportation, restaurants, stores, and hotels. Communities thrive.

The nine major museums in Chicago bring more cash flow to the city each year than do all the major sports teams combined. The museums are gifts (from Julius Rosenwald, among others) that have benefitted all citizens over the past 150 years. Johns Hopkins University is the major employer in the city of Baltimore and the state of Maryland. The land and buildings were gifts of donors and foundations. Physical capital investments are really the gifts that keep on giving over centuries. This tradition continues today at virtually every university, medical center, performance space, and park across the nation. None of these investments meet NCRP's standards for "Philanthropy at Its Best."

Intellectual capital investments from philanthropy are just as compelling. These "donations" launch new ideas. Ideas that are "too innovative" always struggle to find funding. Private investors will usually take only so much risk because they want to be sure of a return on their investment. Government support is even more conservative, as is perfectly wise in that it uses the people's money. But America's foundations feed this entrepreneurial energy precisely because they can be more risk tolerant. The Rockefeller Foundation funded the development of penicillin before the idea of antibiotics even existed. It also funded three young German physicists who had a new idea for a microscope. This investment led to the first electron microscope, the precursor to the astonishing visual-imaging industry of today. Exploratory surgery is a rare event today because doctors can see without using a scalpel first, thanks to freely invested philanthropy that, like the polio vaccine, benefits all people.

Beyond science and technology, American philanthropy has invested in great social ideas as well. When Candy Lightner's daughter was killed by a drunk driver with multiple offenses, she decided to attack the injustice that permitted these manslaughters to continue. Besides many individual donations, small family foundations supported her early efforts. All of us benefit today from the criminalization of drunk driving. This social-justice initiative was the invention of a citizen supported by philanthropy and foundations. Mothers Against Drunk Driving (MADD) and Students Against Drunk Driving (SADD) represent great intellectual capital investments.

Mississippi native James Barksdale, former CEO of FedEx, McCaw Cellular, and then Netscape, donated $100 million to create an institute at his alma mater, the University of Mississippi. Through a partnership among state colleges and the state department of education, it is designed to fund

K–3 literacy programs and to further educate Mississippi K–3 teachers on teaching reading. The Barksdale gift is believed to be the largest donation ever geared solely toward literacy—a human as well as an intellectual capital investment made by a generous American giving back to a cause and to a place that matters to him.

In these cases and countless others, foundation donors stepped in to support risky ideas for changes in science and technology or on social issues. These changes advanced our communities, our society, and our economy. Grassroots communities and minority professionals benefited from these efforts just as the rest of the nation did. These cases of imaginative generosity need to be highlighted in each state. Efforts need to be made to keep encouraging intellectual capital investment across the country.

Human, physical, and intellectual capital investments by philanthropists have made the United States an exceptionally dynamic nation. We cannot afford to dampen this energy by constraining the freedom of donors to make high-risk investments in causes of their own choosing. Curtailing autonomy in philanthropic investments would turn our nation into a less creative, and less desirable, place to live.

Is American-style generosity perfect? Of course not. In a later chapter, I will review the many ways our social-profit sector is working to improve current practices, especially in the work of private foundations. But the record of accomplishment to date argues for sustaining this work as our nation faces a new millennium of challenges.

Many of the creative solutions developed by philanthropic investments have not yet been scaled up to serve the largest possible number of citizens. We all benefit from fewer drunk drivers on the road and from the availability of MRIs and CAT scans. Why do we not also have community literacy programs nationwide or home-health care para-professionals serving their communities across the nation? I wish that Greenlining and NCRP had called for this work.

Could philanthropy do more to address the life conditions of those at the bottom of the nation's economic wealth distribution? Absolutely. Do millions of us benefit from our system of unbounded philanthropy and the ways that it strengthens both democracy and capitalism? Yes. Are there millions who don't get all they need from philanthropy? Yes, and they are our common national concern. They are not the sole concern of their specific advocates. The investments of thousands of foundations and individual donors across the nation attest to this assertion.

Americans struggling to reach the middle class have found wise and committed advocates since the Declaration of Independence was signed. Some, like Jane Addams, working at the end of the nineteenth century, initiated the settlement houses that changed the fate of many hundreds of thousands of immigrants and southern-born African Americans who were drawn to America's northern cities. Others, like Olivia Phelps Stokes, left their entire inheritances to assure the college education of minorities, including Native Americans. Her foundation initiated and funded the United

Negro College Fund. Julius Rosenwald gathered the funds for 5,357 schools throughout the South to educate black children at the beginning of the twentieth century. Foundation donors have a strong record of investing in America's strivers. Today, philanthropists of every race and ethnicity continue this work. John Rogers is funding grassroots public education. Alphonse Fletcher, another successful black financier, is funding his alma maters (Harvard and Yale). Their story is the story of American exceptionalism. The generosity of generations of Americans across races, ethnicities, and religions is a record that no other nation can match.

Part II

A Primer on American Generosity

In this newe land, we must work as one man and abridge ourselves of our superfluities for the supply of each other's necessities.

–John Winthrop,
"A Modell of Christian Charity"

CHAPTER THREE

The Origins of Citizen-to-Citizen Generosity

It is difficult to be a great capitalist and a virtuous, self-disciplined person—remember the parable about the heavily laden camel struggling to enter the city of Jerusalem through the gate known as the "eye of the needle"? It is difficult, but not impossible. Such outstanding people were the citizen-statesmen that the Founders envisioned as leaders of the new nation. Our most notable philanthropists embody just such a profile. They proclaimed this standard in their writings and, more importantly, by their deeds. Best known among them is Andrew Carnegie. His *Gospel of Wealth* lays out the principles to guide a successful capitalist in his civic responsibilities:

> This, then, is held to be the duty of the man of wealth: to set an example of modest, unostenta-

tious living, shunning display or extravagance; to provide moderately for the legitimate wants of those dependent upon him; and, after doing so, to consider all surplus revenues which come to him simply as trust funds, which he is called upon to administer and strictly bound—as a matter of duty—to administer in the manner which, in his judgment, is best calculated to produce the most beneficial results for the community.[1]

How did such ideals emerge in our nation? How did it come to pass that we enjoy a powerful combination of free enterprise and virtuous behavior to power our nation's development? How did this defining American tradition originate? More importantly, what must we do to sustain and enrich this tradition? A brief inquiry into the origins of America's citizen generosity will provide many lessons we can apply to our current philanthropic challenges.

America's early colonists shared a strong commitment to the Judeo-Christian values captured in the story of the Good Samaritan. They were commanded to love God and to "love thy neighbor as thyself." The parable of the Good Samaritan made clear that their neighbors encompassed even those from different tribes and geographies. In 1630, John Winthrop, the head of the Massachusetts Bay Lumber and Fur Trading Company, and eventually governor of the Massachusetts Bay Colony, offered his famous sermon on Christian charity quoted at the start of this chapter.

In his religious idealism, Winthrop envisioned a "city on the hill" built on Christian virtue.* But he was also a practical man with a business to run and investors to repay. He knew full well that the success of the company would depend on mutual respect among the colonists and a willingness to sacrifice for the greater good of the enterprise. Virtuous behavior would be essential to, and inseparable from, business success.

The principled leadership of Winthrop certainly helped the colony to prosper. Mutually beneficial ideas such as barn raisings, potluck meals, and scholarships for gifted but needy students built a sense of shared commitment to everyone's well-being in the community.† We still operate on these same principles today, with bake sales, car washes, and online fundraisers to help families in need get back on their feet.

Prosperity also required independent initiative, of course, and Winthrop saw no conflict with the simultaneous need for interdependence and personal freedom among the people. The drive for prosperity, sparked by the freedom to pursue one's dreams, characterized many colonists who risked their lives crossing the Atlantic. This spirit of personal en-

---

* This ideal refers back to the notion of stewardship, a popular topic among Winthrop's contemporaries, including Rev. William Gouge: "we are not lords of our riches, but stewards; and a steward must give an account of his stewardship." See *A Learned Commentary on the Whole Epistle to the Hebrews*, published posthumously in 1655, http://www.puritanboard.com.

† Ann Radcliffe provided the first scholarships in 1643. Within a decade or so, perhaps a fifth of Harvard students came from the artisan classes and received financial aid. In 1651, the first evidence of annual fund gifts appeared. The artisan families—including farmers, blacksmiths, and candle makers—were making in-kind contributions of grain and other items to the college out of gratitude for the opportunities offered to their sons. Our virtuous cycle began early in our history.

trepreneurship has been documented by a number of distinguished historians.

The historian Edwin J. Perkins estimates that "half of all farm households met the basic qualifications for inclusion in the entrepreneurial category. Few of them may have actually achieved great wealth, but they nonetheless aimed at steadily accumulating productive assets."[2] Perkins describes the self-discipline imposed by colonial farmers and artisans that enabled them to make additional investments in growing larger herds, improving productivity, and developing better markets. He concludes:

> Entrepreneurial attitudes and strategies for upward economic mobility pervaded the free population of the British North American colonies throughout the first two centuries of European settlement. These attributes were shared by the vast majority of colonial households; not only by merchants, but by artisans, most farmers . . . indentured servants, unmarried and still youthful day laborers, and even a few exceptional slaves operating in the urban self-hire market. . . . Historians should henceforth stress that the majority of the free population from colonial times forward were active participants in an economic, social, and political system heavily imbued with entrepreneurial values—a system characterized by high savings rates, a market orientation, and positive attitudes toward the accumulation of wealth.[3]

Chapter Three

The Pulitzer Prize–winning historian Bernard Bailyn describes the motivations of the thousands of British emigrants who paid their own way to America in the years approaching the Revolutionary War: "Almost all, searching rationally for personal betterment or greater security, were, or hoped to be, family-scale entrepreneurs."[4] Entrepreneurship drove the development of new towns and increased land values as roads gradually linked towns and villages.[5] The contemporary champion of these unlimited opportunities was clearly Benjamin Franklin, whose writings are filled with enthusiastic descriptions of success based on hard work, frugality, and, of course, the support of fellow citizens:

> Who then are the kind of Persons to whom an Emigration to America may be advantageous? . . . [H]earty young Labouring Men, who understand the Husbandry of Corn and Cattle . . . may easily establish themselves here. A little Money sav'd of the good Wages they receive here, while they work for others, enables them to buy the land and begin . . . in which they are assisted by the Good-Will of their Neighbors, and some Credit. Multitudes of poor People from England, Ireland, Scotland, and Germany, have by this means in a few years become wealthy Farmers. . . .[6]

In short, as momentum built across the colonies for independence from England, the leaders of the movement recognized two important cultural assets at their disposal: a commitment to mutual support among their fellow colonists and an equally strong commitment to personal enterprise. The challenge would be to unite these values to form a cornerstone for the new nation.

How Did the Founders Establish Our Philanthropic Tradition?

I want to underscore how important understanding our "Founders' intent" is to understanding contemporary philanthropy. The Founders faced countless challenges in crafting a Declaration of Independence that would satisfy the many competing interests among the colonies and the many philosophical and moral differences among the negotiators.[7] The Founders' intent is expressed in the Declaration of Independence. Their language is both philosophical and aspirational. It is philosophical because it defines their belief system, their worldview. It acknowledges a Creator who is active and intentional, making men from their creation equal and endowed with specific rights. The language is aspirational in that real life did not offer such experience even for all white men, never mind others. Both white and black men were indentured servants with neither freedom nor equal rights. So the document expressed the Founders' hopes for the future of America. It gave all citizens something to aspire to. Those most famous words have been the blueprint of freedom and equality for people all over America and all over the world. The words of the Declaration are the American mission statement. To advance that mission statement, citizens would have to be generous and courageous.

As a college president, I used to tell every graduating class that as they expressed their gifts in different lives and professions, as well-educated Americans they had one job description. Their common job was to be gap-closers—closing the gap between the aspirations in the Declaration and the lived experience of their fellow Americans and any others they were privileged to encounter. The Declaration of Independence is the assignment sheet the Founders left to the future. The civil-rights movement, the Polish Solidarity movement, the students facing the tanks in Tiananmen Square—all aimed at making these words a reality in people's lives. The obstacles to their aspirations were often conquered as the people sang our American song: "We Shall Overcome." These facts testify to the power of the Founders' intent.

What Did the Founders Intend?

The Founders wrote and signed some of the most important documents ever written. The undeniable truth remains, however, that certain ones among them exacted a brutal and immoral price for their signatures, and other Founders agreed to pay that price. How can we talk about their commitment to civic virtues like liberty when, in order to win the commitment of Georgia and South Carolina to the Union, the Founders voted to let any state joining the Union re-open their African slave trade from 1776 to 1806? That agreement overturned the earlier vote by the Continental Congress to outlaw the slave trade. It forced more than 40,000 Africans and their descendants to pay the highest price for the Union for another eighty years.

Some commentators have dismissed the Founders for such hypocrisy. Others have concluded that most were firmly opposed to slavery and set the Union on a path to end it expeditiously.[8] Still others barely acknowledge any flaw in the decisions they made.[9] Clearly, however, some of the Founders were so committed to slavery that they would have sacrificed the Union to maintain it. Thus, we must pause and recognize the irreconcilable moral conflict they encountered.

The anti-slavery Founders faced a choice between launching the Union at the price of expanding a heinous evil—slavery—and failing in their appointed task. Despite widely differing lives and moral views, this group of men shared a commitment to forging the Union. Their commitment to personal liberty meant that the perpetuation of human bondage could not permanently co-exist with the principles in the Declaration. While there was indeed a painful period of coexistence, slavery did not endure. The principles of the Declaration have. Many Americans, particularly African Americans, have paid a terrible price over the years sustaining the fight for justice and equality for all through the civil-rights movement.

The historian William Freehling suggests that the Founders' strategy was to restrict slavery where restriction could be managed and to tolerate it where opposition could destroy the Union, believing (hoping) that this approach would end slavery over time. Freehling contends that both views are misleading. He writes: "The abolitionist process proceeded slowly but inexorably from 1776 to 1860; slowly in part because of what Jefferson and his contemporaries did not do, inexorably in part because of what they did."[10]

As the nation's president, Jefferson wrote to Congress in 1806 alerting them to the approach of the period when

> you may interpose your authority constitutionally to stop Americans from all further participation in those violations of human rights which have been so long continued on the unoffending inhabitants of Africa, and which the morality, the reputation, and the best interests of our country have long been eager to proscribe. . . . [T]he reform, if passed in 1807, could make certain that no extra African was dragged legally across the seas.[11]

Without the Union, abolition would have been even less likely. This issue is still highly contested, but Freehling has the right idea, in my judgment. He acknowledges the Founders' flaws, while insisting that these leaders "drastically reduced the slavocracy's potential area, population, and capacity to endure."[12] Slaveholding gradually weakened in the North, and anti-slavery forces began to press for the change that finally took hold with the adoption of the Thirteenth Amendment in 1865. The Founders also eliminated slavery in the lands governed by the Northwest Ordinance.

The Founders' strategy did not advance the end of slavery as rapidly as most twenty-first-century Americans now wish, but they accomplished their work at a time when commitments to human rights were vastly weaker all over the world than they are today. Consider the conclusion of Julian Bond, the black activist, legislator, and longtime head of the NAACP. Bond "showed how Jefferson's words in the Declaration of Independence could be invoked to transcend—or overlook—Jefferson's bigotry. In Bond's interpretation, the true Jeffersonian legacy was the best one, the one that surmounted his own parochialism, racism, and slaveholding."[13] His words have mattered most.

The document that the Founders finally agreed to sign has provided the basis for countless additional documents affirming human rights all over the globe since 1776. Americans can revere the Founders for the courageous and pragmatic decisions they made on behalf of the Republic in such morally treacherous times. White Americans also need to recognize that other Americans may not view this history in quite the same way. All Americans should regret that the ancestors of many African Americans paid a very high price so that the Founders' decisions could yield the Union. We need to acknowledge the sacrifices of our enslaved ancestors and to keep working for justice and opportunity for all.

The rest of the Founders' story may be more profound in light of the history of the Founders and slavery. Despite their differences, they recognized that success for a new republic, in which the laws of the land applied equally to all citizens, required both individual enterprise and mutual support among citizens. They ultimately engineered a successful synthesis of these two potentially antithetical notions, and in so doing they built the foundation of our citizen-to-citizen philanthropy.

Many of the Founders were well-educated and visionary men. They wanted to base a new republic on the very best ideas produced by educated minds, great principles such as justice and equality before the law. David McCullough goes so far as to declare that they were "marinated" in the classics.[14] They had studied the classical and contemporary European political theorists: Aristotle, Machiavelli, and, perhaps most importantly, Montesquieu.* They were anxious to differentiate the new nation from the tired European system that extended legacy powers and privileges to the landed gentry across many generations. But a new government also had to enable asset formation and the emergence of a strong economy. This meant ensuring that individual entrepreneurs were free to amass real wealth. Wealth would be critically important to improving the quality of life for all, and also to enabling the country to defend itself against its likely competitors—global behemoths like England and France.

The revolutionary planners were starting at a distinct disadvantage in this competition. The colonies did not approach the levels of wealth, sophistication, and material comfort that numbers of Europeans were enjoying. The colonies

---

* The baron (1689–1754), a French lawyer, is best known for the idea that dividing government up into branches that could check each other's authority was the best way to avoid despotism, an idea developed in *The Spirit of the Laws*.

were clinging to the fringe of Western civilization in 1770, and most of the Founders recognized this. They were familiar with the accomplishments of the great European scientists Newton and Galileo, architects Palladio and Wren, and polymath philosophers like Descartes (who also refined lens grinding to make telescopes and microscopes) and Pascal (whose work in geometry and number theory remains as fundamental as his theological writings). Haydn and Mozart were dazzling audiences with their refined brilliance. These men defined the "modern" world.

The first European university was established in 1088 at Bologna. Then in 1090 the University of Paris was founded, followed by Oxford in 1096, Cambridge in 1209, and Salamanca in 1218. Thirty-eight major universities had been created in Europe before Columbus discovered America. These institutions had educated the researchers whose work kindled the Renaissance and the scientists and mathematicians who had engineered the Newtonian revolution. By the middle of the eighteenth century, the Enlightenment—that great expansion of human reasoning in fields as diverse as optics, agriculture, and medicine—was in full bloom.

The colonies could not compete with such intellectual accomplishments, nor could they match the economic power of the French, Spanish, Dutch, and English monarchies that sent explorers around the world and established successful global trading routes. They could not compete in shipbuilding, global import-export businesses, or manufacturing. England had dominated the textile industry since the late 1600s and was beginning to mechanize it. Richard Arkwright invented the spinning frame that used water power for spinning in 1767. How could the colonies compete with, let alone defend themselves against, these formidable nations?

Daily life for most of the American population was still more about subsistence than wealth-building. Urban life, in particular, was severely underdeveloped. Sanitary systems illustrate the disparity. The first vaulted, stone-walled sewer system was built in Paris in the 1300s. It developed over centuries and reached a level of complexity such that the civil engineer Pierre Bruneseau, the Jules Verne of the Paris sewers, required seven years simply to complete a basic inspection and maintenance cycle. Until about 1840, American cities lacked sewer systems entirely. The first ones built were based, of course, upon European models.

America needed economic development, especially robust commercial enterprises that would create better transportation, sanitation, and infrastructure. The colonies needed to produce higher-quality goods, from ships to textiles, for domestic consumers as well as for export. The Founders needed more than a set of high-minded principles: they needed to do everything in their power to encourage free enterprise and wealth accumulation. Launching new enterprises would be expensive and would require years of investment before they could turn a profit.

The Founding Fathers addressed the issue of private property directly in the Constitution. They understood that the creators of great ideas should control their intellectual property in the "newe land." Their ingenious solution to this issue is our patent law system, which is outlined in the Constitution. It is remarkable that these detailed protections for inventors are outlined in such a sweeping document, but this fact underscores the Founders' concern with promoting economic creativity and entrepreneurship. Their system has worked remarkably well for hundreds of years, despite the fact that they could scarcely have imagined the technologies and processes that their framework now covers.

The patent system recognizes the right of an individual to profit from his or her invention, and it offers protections and legal remedies should another party attempt to profit unfairly from a patented invention. However, the Founders recognized that society as a whole also had an interest in learning from these private innovations. Too much secrecy would retard the march of intellectual (and commercial) progress. So protections were offered only to those who disclosed the details of their inventions in publicly available documents (patents), thus enabling interested parties to study the new ideas and perhaps build on them for future innovations.* The term of the patent protection was limited to a fixed period, providing ample time for the inventor to develop and profit from his or her invention. At a point in the future, however, the new idea would enter the public domain and be available to all without charge.

---

* The Constitution gives Congress the power "to promote the progress of science and useful arts, by securing for limited times to authors and inventors the exclusive right to their respective writings and discoveries." Article I, section 8, paragraph 8.

The Founders adopted a similar solution for another potential area of conflict between public and private interests: intellectual property created by artists and writers. Here the solution was copyright law, which enabled the private creator to maintain ownership, again for a fixed period of time. This idea had originated in Britain in the early-eighteenth century (the 1710 Statute of Anne), and had fixed the term of ownership for the creator of artistic property at twenty-eight years.

The Founders argued at some length about the proper term for copyright protection. Most were naturally opposed to any arrangements "in perpetuity," as this presumably reminded them of the mechanisms by which European aristocrats had maintained family lands and fortunes for generations, to the disadvantage of the larger populace. Jefferson was particularly outspoken on the issue of perpetuity. He wrote to Madison on September 6, 1789: "I set out on this ground which I suppose to be self evident, 'that the earth belongs in usufruct to the living;' that the dead have neither powers nor rights over it."[15]

Jefferson lobbied for a nineteen-year term, but in the end the Constitution specifies only that copyright applies for a "limited term."* So the concept of intellectual property serves commercial and democratic ends and both private and public interests. Over time, the private wealth of human imagination becomes part of the common wealth available to

---

* A copyright can be inherited from the owner upon his or her death, but cannot be extended by the heirs. See Lewis Hyde, "Advantage Google," *New York Times Book Review*, October 4, 2009.

enrich the nation as a whole. Madison called the arrangement "a compensation (to the creator) for a benefit actually gained to the community."[16]

These carefully reasoned clauses of the Constitution provide a window into the preoccupation of the Founders with achieving a fair balance between private and public interests. They were well aware that the unfettered pursuit of private wealth, as vital as this might be to the prosperity of the nation, ran the risk of "unbalancing" these interests. Wealth, they had reason to fear, could overwhelm the virtues in the citizenry that were deemed necessary for democracy to operate effectively. To quote a contemporary scholar, "The generation of the American Revolution believed that the success of their experiment in republican government required male self-control."[17]

Bernard Bailyn notes that the Founders were strongly focused on the need to manage self-interest and corruption in the fragile experiment in self-governance that they aspired to establish. The Founders were aware of the lessons of history that taught how republics were dependent on virtues such as "simplicity, patriotism, integrity, a love of justice and of liberty" among the citizenry.[18] Bailyn notes that Montesquieu, echoing Aristotle, contended that democracy needed a more virtuous citizenry than did a monarchy, because in a popular government, "the person entrusted with the execution of the laws is sensible of his being subject to their direction."[19]

John Adams, Benjamin Rush, and Thomas Jefferson all worried about the effect of burgeoning wealth on men's virtue, starting with its impact on their self-discipline. They recognized the importance of protecting entrepreneurs' chances for wealth, but they worried that commercial success might encourage greed. Such an eventuality would risk a rapid decline into a tyranny of wealth in the new republic.

The conflict between freedom and virtue was the core challenge of the architects of the new nation. Classical authors taught that the virtues of prudence, justice, fortitude, and temperance were essential. Franklin's more homey virtues—honesty, thrift, and simplicity—seemed equally important to a just republic. In short, democratic government required a widely practiced set of civic virtues that would bind citizens, and especially their leaders, to a shared concern for the common good in the context of individual freedom.

Some participants in the debates felt that these high-minded ideals of civic humanism were a luxury that America could not afford. After all, most of the thinkers who had pushed these ideas, from Aristotle to Montesquieu, had little experience in the rough-and-tumble competitive world of commerce. And it was largely the economic issues of taxation without representation, of unfair tariffs and the like, that had driven the colonists to the brink of war. So the negotiation process for the Founders turned again and again on the quest for balance between competing goods, the protection of individual freedoms, and the habits of citizenship that would protect the public good. This tension is not unlike the tension we face today in the world of philanthropy.

A Brief Detour through the Scottish Enlightenment

I want to add an important side trip to this brief tour through the Founders' efforts to create a union. As important as their classical educations were, the Founders owe a special debt to Scottish thinkers concerning the principles that make American citizen generosity a success. Many of the Founders were familiar with the problem of seemingly incompatible goods— i.e., the essential preservation of individual freedom *and* the maintenance of virtuous behavior in society—because they knew that the leaders of Scotland had wrestled with this very issue during the preceding decades. Many of our founding statesmen knew the history of Scotland and the recent Scottish Enlightenment, which was marked by great economic and social progress. Thomas Jefferson, Alexander Hamilton, Henry Knox (first secretary of war), Edmund Randolph (first attorney general), and George Washington were all of Scottish ancestry. Nine of the thirteen governors of the original colonies shared Scottish roots, including Patrick Henry of Virginia. Jefferson's tutors were Scottish. Franklin had traveled extensively through Scotland in 1759 and maintained an active correspondence with the scholars in Edinburgh before and after his second visit in 1771.

Benjamin Rush, another signer of the Declaration, studied medicine at the University of Edinburgh, graduating in 1768. This was the very year that he succeeded in convincing that university's famous leader—a conservative, broad-minded theologian named John Witherspoon—to leave Scotland and accept the presidency of Princeton University, Rush's (and

Madison's) alma mater. Witherspoon embraced the belief that all men are innately moral, able to distinguish right from wrong and inclined toward the former. He saw a well-trained mind as an asset in this process and encouraged his students to debate with those who disagreed with this view, including the renegade thinker and Witherspoon's fellow Scot, David Hume. Witherspoon became a signer of the Declaration and an influential member of the Continental Congress while continuing to lead Princeton.

The Founders identified many parallels between the circumstances of Scotland in the late-seventeenth and early-eighteenth centuries and the American colonies in the eighteenth. One hundred years earlier, Scotland had been situated at the fringe of the then-civilized world. As one historian described those early days: "The backwardness of the Highland economy is almost impossible to exaggerate: The wheel was a novelty until the eighteenth century in parts of Scotland."* From 1690 to the early years of the eighteenth century, Scotland experienced several very bad harvests; mass starvation ensued. Scotland lost an estimated 15 percent of its population. Its financial sector neared collapsed in 1700, when only twelve of its forty-seven joint-stock companies had survived the recession. British navigation laws severely restricted Scottish trade. British taxes made Scottish coal, salt, and linens too expensive to market competitively, and its foreign trade

---

* "When a cart appeared in East Kilbride, twelve miles from Glasgow, in 1723, the crowds collected round so wonderful a machine: it might have been a satellite from the moon." Hugh Trevor-Roper, "The Scottish Enlightenment," *Studies on Voltaire and the 18th Century* 58 (1967): 1650.

dropped precipitously. Something needed to be done. This is how Daniel Howe frames the question:

> The intellectual agenda of the thinkers of the Scottish Enlightenment was set by the practical issues of their time and place. . . . Scottish intellectuals felt acutely conscious of their provincialism and were both defensive about it and anxious to overcome it. This marginal status seems to have spurred them to achievement, as it has so many other people. Most important of all, the glaring contrasts they encountered between sophisticated prosperity and primitive backwardness provoked Scottish intellectuals into serious reflection on the nature of social and economic progress.[20]

These thinkers went to work on the vexing challenge of free enterprise. If the Scots were fortunate enough to escape their poverty—and with it the tyranny of the British—through a system of unfettered individual freedom, what was to prevent a new form of tyranny, the tyranny of the wealthy, from coming to dominate their nation? Thoughtful leadership and principled behavior would be required of all citizens to reach their goal: the greatest amount of happiness for the largest number of citizens.

These knotty questions drew the attention of the moral philosophers of the time, and happily the nation was blessed with a number of outstanding thinkers. Francis Hutcheson of Glasgow was among the most influential. Hutcheson was an optimistic man, committed like Witherspoon to a view of mankind as inherently moral. He believed that the study of classical thinkers, as well as Christian writers, would advance one's ability to act virtuously, even while enjoying the greatest personal freedoms and wealth-building opportunities. Liberty was essential to the pursuit of happiness, but the source of happiness, he argued, ultimately resided in helping others to achieve happiness.

Hutcheson's most famous student was Adam Smith, author of the *Theory of Moral Sentiments* and the better-known *Wealth of Nations*. Smith has achieved iconic status as the first modern economist and champion of free enterprise through thoughts such as these, in the *Wealth of Nations*:

> The natural effort of every individual to better his own condition . . . is so powerful a principle that it is alone, not only capable of carrying on the society to wealth and prosperity, but of surmounting a hundred impertinent obstructions with which the folly of human laws too often incumbers its operations.[21]

Yet this champion of free enterprise was not a partisan of the skeptical David Hume, who had provocatively written that "reason is, and ought to be, the slave of the passions." Smith remained a loyal student of Hutcheson. He thought of himself as a moral philosopher intent upon bridging the gap between his teacher's (naïve) optimism and the skepticism of his opponents. Smith proposed a bridge in his *Theory of Moral Sentiments*. He asserted: "[V]irtue is upon all ordinary occasions, even with regards to this life, real wisdom, and the surest and readiest means of obtaining both safety and advantage."

Smith theorized that we have the capacity to discern the reactions of our fellow humans to our behavior and to be shaped by these reactions. Moreover, we also have the ability to "reflect," that is, to judge ourselves both as others see us and as we see ourselves. We know what we admire in others—honesty, generosity, compassion—and we are capable of seeing ourselves against these standards. This play of imagination defines our moral essence and intensifies our concern for others and our solidarity with them. Any action on our part, whether by omission or commission, that impinges on the happiness of the other necessarily reflects painfully back on us (and our happiness) when we observe it through the eyes of the other.

This synthesis of freedom and responsibility made Smith famous long before he wrote the *Wealth of Nations*. Smith was certainly an opponent of government interventions that upset the level playing field of economic enterprise. His famous articulation of an "invisible hand" in the marketplace is simply a restatement of this belief, prompted by his hostility toward the onerous taxation and tariff policies that the English government imposed on Scotland. But his importance to our culture of citizen generosity cannot be overlooked. Smith's "invisible hand" was a product of virtuous hearts and minds making the marketplace. By focusing on the interdependence of citizens in a democratic society, he restored a good deal of the idealism and optimism of his teacher Francis Hutcheson.

This rapid and selective overview cannot not do justice to the complexity of the Scottish Enlightenment. I simply want to underscore that the practical merchants of Glasgow and the academic thinkers of Edinburgh developed some important strategies to enhance the well-being of their nation, strategies that bridged their philosophical differences. They agreed, for instance, on the essential need for an educated citizenry. The Parliament of Scotland voted to establish locally funded, church-supervised schools in every parish in the country in 1696. By the end of the 1700s, Scotland had the highest literacy rates in Europe.

The Scots also developed a system of citizen societies devoted to identifying ideas for advancing the nation. The Honorable Society of Improvers was established in 1723. It was the first society focused on sharing ways to progress. It focused on improving agriculture. In 1725, Alexander Monro (1697–1767) helped launch the Society for the Improvement of Medical Knowledge, with the goal of rivaling the medical care offered in London and Leiden. This society broadened its scope after 1745 and became the Society for Improving Philosophy and Natural Knowledge (science), or the Philosophical Society, and eventually the Royal Society of Edinburgh in 1783.

Monro belonged to several societies: the original Honorable Society of Improvers of the Knowledge of Agriculture in Scotland, the Select Society, and the Edinburgh Society for Encouraging Arts, Sciences, Manufactures, and Agriculture in Scotland, an offshoot of the Select Society.* The Select Society brought together thinkers like Adam Smith, David Hume, and Colin MacLaurin—the mathematician and engineer whose work on geometry and calculus, and whose commentary on Newton's physics, made him one of the leading scholars in his field. He used his mathematical research to lay a sound foundation for actuarial tables to be used by the insurance industry. His work helped assure a decent life for widows and children of ministers and professors.

The societies created convenient ways for the members to advance each other's knowledge and contributions to productivity. Adam Smith became a sponsor of James Watt when the latter set up as a mathematical-instrument maker in Glasgow. Smith sponsored other men in advancing an academy of design and in establishing a type foundry. Each of these efforts built trust among the members, expanded human potential, and raised expectations for further improvements.

Smith's efforts with Watt eventuated in Watt's refinement of the steam engine in 1769 in Glasgow. Watt developed the dominant design for the steam engine with funding from the English venture capitalist Matthew Boulton. Patent protec-

---

* Monro proved to be a remarkable citizen-leader. His range of involvement in his community was remarkable. Besides teaching and practicing medicine, he was a manager of the Royal Infirmary and a director of the Bank of Scotland. In addition, he served as a justice of the peace, a manager of the orphans hospital and of the Scheme (pension plan) for the Widows of Ministers and Professors.

tion was provided by the Scottish Parliament. Watt's engine transformed the coal-mining industry, and then steel-making. It was pivotal to the launch of the Industrial Revolution.

The "improvement society" strategy worked. Linen production and trade increased seven-fold between 1730 and 1790. The same scale of improvement occurred in the tobacco trade. The Scottish share of British trade rose from 10 percent in 1738 to 52 percent in 1769. Populations grew in all the major cities by over 25 percent in the fifty years from 1751 to 1800. Monro's work made Scottish medicine the envy of Europe.

This stunning progress did not go unnoticed. In 1762, the famous French writer and social critic Voltaire praised this land as a pinnacle of "enlightenment." He noted: "We look to Scotland for all our ideas of civilization."[22] Quite a change in standing and achievement!

The leadership thinkers of this era in Scotland integrated civic responsibility with economic development: "The Scottish Enlightenment, then, consisted of a self-conscious band of programmatic intellectuals . . . seeking to enlist private wealth on the side of their country's public good."[23]

Their synthesis embraced empiricism, efficiency, utility, and maximization of quantifiable returns. These ideas were the fruits of human reason, and human reason was the most powerful tool to advance human well-being. Because well-being required the largest amount of happiness for the largest number of people, the Scottish leaders were persuaded that "human reason could indeed integrate the productive values, the civic virtues, and personal liberty through a dedication to human flourishing."*

The Scots' famous practicality convinced them that civic humanism would have to include what was good for a fair civil society *and* for a robust economy, for the individual *and* the community. They argued that the virtues required of successful merchants and businessmen were the same as those expected of society in general. Prudence, justice, fortitude, temperance, generosity, thrift, and self-discipline, along with efficiency and utility, would make the republic and its businesses work better. Private virtue was not an abstraction at odds with productive action. In a flourishing republic, it would function as an essential component of the rule of law.

Why does all this matter to us in America? The relevance becomes clear when we consider our tradition of citizen-to-citizen generosity as a product of this very synthesis of virtue and enterprise. "In America, the Scottish Enlightenment came to a kind of fulfillment denied it at home. . . . In the America of the revolutionary generation, by contrast, the leading intellectuals were the statesmen."[24]

---

* Ryan Patrick Hanley, "Social Science and Human Flourishing: The Scottish Enlightenment and Today," *Journal of Scottish Philosophy* 7, no. 1 (2009): 29–46. The story of the Rev. Henry Duncan perfectly illustrates this pragmatic integration. After studying at Edinburgh, Duncan became the pastor of a poor rural church in the west of Scotland, where he promoted employment opportunities for his worshippers and created a savings bank for their use while writing moral tracts and running a "friendly society" (an early life-insurance cooperative). See George John C. Duncan, *Memoir of the Rev. Henry Duncan, D.D. of Ruthwell* (Edinburgh: William Oliphant and Sons, 1848), 95–96.

The Scottish strategy of collaboration across fields—grounded in moral philosophy—inspired the American Founders. They explored the virtue-driven, but thoroughly practical, ideas and structures that had shown benefit in Scotland, and they designed these into our Declaration and our Constitution.[25]

America's Founders worked together until they too had developed a strong synthesis of apparently opposing "goods"—freedom, virtue, and enterprise. Today, we are all beneficiaries of their wisdom and courage. The outcome of the synthesis of civic humanism and economic development in America is summarized in the expression "self-interest, rightly understood." Citizens must understand that they serve their own best interests by working in the best interest of their fellow citizens.

The wording of the Declaration of Independence reveals the Founders' commitment to blending civic humanism and economic wealth-building. The original draft called for the right to "life, liberty, and property" (that is, direct ownership). Property ownership was, after all, a tangible, measurable activity, one that would have appealed to the strongest partisans of wealth-building. And it would certainly have been easier to enforce as a right than the almost fanciful promise of the final draft: a right to "the pursuit of happiness"! But in this case, we can see the direct influence of Hutcheson and Smith. This turn of phrase had come to represent, in their writings, the ideal synthesis of personal liberty and concern for fellow citizens. A government guided by "We, the People" would pursue this ideal, and seek to bind Americans together in this task throughout our history.

> We hold these truths to be self-evident . . . That all men are created equal; that they are endowed by their Creator with certain unalienable rights; that among these are life, liberty, and the pursuit of happiness; that, to secure these rights, governments are instituted among men, deriving their just powers from the consent of the governed. . . .

This vision established an entirely different set of relationships among individual citizens and between citizens and their government than in the monarchies of Europe. There would be little use in America for those wishing to behave as passive subjects. The path was set for a government of and by the people. The purpose of such a government is clear—to secure the rights of life, liberty, and the pursuit of happiness for all men. In their Declaration, the Founders engaged all of us, as members of the government, in this awesome task. Citizens would be expected to contribute their personal qualities, their productive energies, and their virtuous behavior to build the society that the Declaration announced. They would have to accept personal responsibility for themselves *and* for the well-being of others. This is still our responsibility as citizens today.

The Founders committed us to both independence and interdependence. The signers recognized the significant gap between the great words of their Declaration (and eventually the Constitution of 1787) and the lived experience of those residing in the new republic. Slavery continued. But ultimately the ideals have defeated the injustices.

The Declaration is a homework assignment, a to-do list for American citizens. It is not a bill of rights (that came later), but rather a visionary statement that commits each of us to reduce that gap between the ideals on which the nation was founded and the day-to-day lived experience of fellow citizens. We are the people responsible for seeing that the laws of the land apply equally to all citizens. This has been the work of the abolitionists and civil-rights marchers, those opposing child labor and those welcoming immigrants, those advocating for the poor and those pursuing universal suffrage. This is the basis of our American philanthropic tradition.

Generosity in Action

An audacious vision is only as valuable as the plan to achieve it is effective. The Founders' ideals of equal rights and responsibilities provided an audacious vision, but it required a strategy to be fulfilled. The Founders' approach worked better than they themselves probably imagined. Their plan led directly to the creation of our unique social-profit sector.

How could the newly born republic assure strong economic development and the practice of virtue—particularly male self-control—in a newly independent society? At least some of the Founders saw the women of the new republic as an important asset in sustaining virtue.

John Adams got a sharp reminder from home about the male self-control issue as he worked on the Declaration. In her March 31, 1776, letter, his wife, Abigail, wrote:

> I long to hear that you have declared an independency, and by the way in the new Code of Laws which I suppose it will be necessary to make I desire that you would Remember the Ladies, and be more generous and favorable to them than your ancestors. Do not put such unlimited power into the hands of the Husbands. *Remember all Men would be tyrants if they could.* If particular care and attention is not paid to the Ladies we are determined to ferment a Rebellion, and will not hold ourselves bound by any Laws in which we have no voice, or Representation.[26]

Abigail did not get her wish for representation, but that is hardly surprising. The social role of women was a problematic issue in early America, which was reliant on an English common-law tradition that limited the role of women to the domestic scene. But Adams and his colleagues faced plenty of skepticism about a government by the people, given the abundant evidence of human weakness—especially among the male of the species. So they crafted a way to "remember the ladies," although not in the way Abigail Adams had in mind.

The Founders were able to agree that women were uniquely suited to exert their moral authority in domestic settings and to instill virtue in their children. As is still the case today, most people believed that the earlier children are taught self-discipline and virtuous behavior, the more likely it is that these teachings will shape their characters as adults. Benjamin Rush tells us that "the first impressions upon the minds of children are generally derived from women."[27]

Rush* laid out his thinking, carefully working around the issue of direct enfranchisement: "The equal share that every citizen has in liberty and the possible share he may have in the government of the country make it necessary that our ladies should be qualified to a certain degree by a peculiar and suitable education, to concur in instructing their sons in the principles of liberty and government."[28]

So in their patriarchal wisdom, the Founders invested their hopes for civic humanism in their natural allies at home. A republican mother could "perpetuate the republic by her refusal to countenance lovers who were not devoted to the service of the state, and by commitment to raise sons who were educated for civic virtue and for responsible citizenship. They would also raise self-reliant daughters who, in their turn, would raise republican sons."†

A woman's physical and intellectual efforts should be dedicated to the maintenance and morality of her family and

---

* I should state that Rush, while noted for his support of women's education, wasn't a huge populist. He thought education would make women better companions for their husbands, but that education should remain a luxury item for select members of society. See Abraham Blinderman, *Three Early Champions of Education* (Bloomington: Indiana University Press, 1976), 23.

† Linda K. Kerber, *No Constitutional Right to Be Ladies* (New York: Hill and Wang, 1999), 146. Kerber does not view this male perspective as particularly respectful of women's potential contribution to the nation, but more a matter of convenience.

community. The responsibilities of republican motherhood appeared to hold women effectively within this domestic framework. But this proved to be one of the Founders' few miscalculations.

Despite the constraints in colonial women's lives, the opportunity to contribute to the future of the republic energized a certain number of women to think expansively. "I expect to see our young women forming a new era in female history," wrote Judith Sargent Murray in 1798.[29] A certain Miss Jackson, upon graduation from a girls' academy, waxed more eloquent:

> A woman who is skilled in every useful art, who practices every domestic virtue, may by her example inspire her brothers, her husband, or her son with such a love of virtue, such just ideas of the true value of civil liberty, that future heroes and statesmen, who arrive at the summit of military or political fame shall exultingly declare, it is to my mother I own this elevation.[30]

I doubt whether the Founders anticipated how their hopes for republican motherhood would play out across American history. Did they remember that virtue cannot be taught through uplifting readings and maternal exhortations alone? Mothers know that children learn good behaviors when they see them practiced. How could a mother explain the command to "love your neighbor" if she marched her children to church past a poor widow and her little ones looking for food in the town square? Inevitably, the town square became that mother's classroom. And from there, as we will see, courageous women continued to expand their mandate in the public sphere, creating the social-profit sector of today.

How did these republican mothers model virtuous behavior? Handouts to the destitute might fulfill the definition of Christian charity and were undoubtedly an important starting point in the education of children. But an additional kind of virtue was required for a successful democracy. A civil society depends on the self-reliance and industriousness of each citizen, and simple charity does not address these wider civic concerns. So republican mothers needed to envision and model additional virtues. The women began to assemble themselves and to create small local female societies.[31]

The earliest women's societies were initiated before the end of the eighteenth century. In some ways they borrowed their ideals and strategies from the Scottish improvement societies of the previous century. The Society for the Relief of the Distressed launched in Philadelphia in 1795, and the Society for the Relief of Poor Widows with Small Children in New York in 1797. The colorful names of these groups reveal the limited, targeted missions their organizers aspired to fill. My personal favorite: the Female Association for the Relief of the Sick Poor, and for the Education of Such Female Children as Do Not Belong to, or Are Not Provided for by, Any Religious Society.

The Society for the Relief of Poor Widows with Small Children taught mothers to make shirts and then sold them to benefit widows. Some societies were called "cent societies" because women came with a weekly donation of a penny for dues, their contribution from their own household budgets. Other societies sponsored the ambitious idea of houses of industry. These women established houses with multiple apartments where spouseless women could live with their children. The houses had rooms for spinning wheels, looms, and other equipment for the women's work. They also had rooms where volunteers cared for the children while their mothers worked. Decades later, the settlement-house movement would reinvent similar solutions for newly arrived immigrant families.

The Female Society for Relief and Employment for the Poor and others also demonstrated both competence and creativity when it came to fundraising. Dues payments by members were the most common source of support, with some groups permitting men to become honorary members if they paid dues (and if they promised not to participate in meetings!). Women also set up subscription drives throughout their cities to raise more money.

Such actions respected the families in need, giving them opportunities, not handouts. This form of assistance would be preferable to straight charity, except in emergencies. The women could alleviate poverty, sustain the dignity and independence of the poor widow, *and* teach all the children—hers and theirs—generosity, compassion, frugality, and industriousness. Effective teaching at home was linked to social transformations in the community. In this sense, republican motherhood birthed American social entrepreneurship. Remarkably, women succeeded in this task many generations before they were allowed to own property in their own names or work outside of their own homes.

The Synthesis

The Founders' intent was to craft a government of free citizens that would encourage individual enterprise in the context of "self-interest, rightly understood." They articulated a synthesis that would advance both of these "goods," resulting in prosperity and happiness for the greatest number of citizens. Given the traditions of industry and mutual support among the colonists, the negotiating skills of the Founders, and the natural resources of America, there was reason for optimism. The contribution of women to the transmission of values necessary to sustain the new republic also provided an essential component of American prosperity, and a key to American exceptionalism.

Citizen-to-citizen generosity is the vital link between civic humanism and economic development. Philanthropy depends on the donor's economic success, no matter how modest, and on that donor's recognition of "self-interest, rightly understood." A donor must recognize that his economic success has been enabled by others, either directly or indirectly (by ensuring a stable and secure environment, for instance). This debt is acknowledged through gratitude that, in turn, inspires generosity. Thus, philanthropy engages citizens in each others' well-being. The Founders' pragmatism is easy to see. Virtue and economic success are linked for the donor and for the recipient. Both are basic to the lives of citizens in a democratic republic.

In this framework, we see the weaving together of the strands that create our civic fabric: our optimism, our entrepreneurism, our founding documents, and our citizenry engaged in voluntary philanthropy and in private wealth-building. This dynamic process has kept a dangerous enemy—cynicism—from the door. Even in the worst times for the civil-rights movement, Martin Luther King, Jr., reached out to the founding documents and to the words of Jefferson to remind us of the promises the Founders committed us to keep for all citizens. The success of our free-enterprise system has enabled millions of citizens to become donors and to expand the great tradition of generosity that began with Ann Radcliffe's donation of scholarship funds to Harvard in 1643.

What Is the Lesson for Today from Our Founding Fathers?

This brief history is worth knowing because it is easy to take for granted the remarkable balance the Founders achieved in our founding documents. This is especially true now that the United States has defined the modern world for more than a century. Oliver Wendell Holmes said: "Historic continuity with the past is not a duty, it is only a necessity."[32] The Founders' story is our story, just as theirs was, in large measure, the story of the Scottish Enlightenment. The Founders' success in adapting the Scots' practical synthesis of freedom and virtue should speak to all of us today. America has succeeded by calling on our best selves to find the best outcomes for the largest numbers of citizens. Any attempt to unbalance this thoughtful synthesis betrays our Founders' intent for the new nation.

Legislating virtue is wrong for us because it short circuits our mutuality as fellow citizens. In the current controversy over legislative intervention, I believe that we should be guided by the Founders' intent for a practical synthesis of competing goods. Understanding the challenges they faced and the compromises they reached should guide our thinking today. In short, let's be practical.

Practicality works for Americans. I believe that Americans who embrace the Founders' intent will respond to an open invitation to develop citizen-based, citizen-funded approaches to helping fellow citizens in need. The challenges facing many citizens who aspire to the security of middle-class life in America need to be addressed by citizens, and especially by those with the power and funds to improve the systems designed to support this journey, from education and health care to employment and affordable housing.

A Statesman

- A person of either gender who moves from principles of honesty, integrity, justice, generosity, compassion, courage, patience, and frugality in making decisions that affect himself, his own community, and the wider community around him. Statesmen consider actions in their impact over time rather than only in their immediate contexts.

- A person willing to take responsibility for the greater good and operate from civic virtues that are the statesman's principles.

- A person with great responsibility and some power who is motivated to lead beyond his self-interest and for the larger benefit of others. Historical examples are: Ben Franklin, Thomas Jefferson, Abigail Adams, John Adams, Catherine Ferguson, John Jay, Esther DeBerdt Reid, Thurgood Marshall, Mary McCloud Bethune, and Dwight Eisenhower.

- Statesmen have the capacity to operate in all settings from the position of "self-interest, rightly understood." This concept is quintessentially American. Our democracy requires statesmen in all walks of life if our way of life is to perdure.

Foundation boards should resist efforts to have their institutions replace government support for basic social services at the expense of funding experimentation and innovation because it suggests that philanthropic dollars are interchangeable with public tax dollars.

–Emmett Carson, Ph.D.,
"Current Challenges to Foundation Board Governance:
A Worst Case Scenario or The Perfect Storm?"

CHAPTER FOUR

Citizen-to-Citizen Generosity in Action: American Private Foundations

The Founders' vision for the new nation depended on wealth-generating private enterprise and a self-disciplined and generous (i.e., virtuous) citizenry. Our millions of social-profit organizations testify to the success of their plans. The great number of citizens who contribute their hard-earned dollars to support these organizations proves that the virtue of generosity is alive and well. This combination has produced an American trifecta: our representative democracy, our market-driven economy, and our citizen-led social-profit sector. The Founders would be proud, and a little bit in awe, of their success as practical visionaries.

The private foundation is a unique and essential component of this social-profit sector. As the Founders had hoped, private enterprise—driven by hard work, determination, and optimism—produced considerable individual wealth. These efforts were greatly aided as the government provided a secure and stable environment for investment. Wealthy men embraced the ideals set forth in our Declaration and elected to dedicate significant portions of their accumulated wealth to causes that would benefit their communities. This process began remarkably quickly after the founding of the nation and continues to this day.

The private foundation has served as a popular vehicle for well-to-do citizens to organize and manage these commitments. Such structures have grown in popularity in the late-twentieth century, along with the numbers of wealthy individuals. While private foundations contribute only a small portion of the combined annual budgets of all social-profit organizations, their impact is highly significant.* Large foundations provide a high degree of visibility to the organizations they fund. They also have the ability, through their special legal status, to make long-term commitments to causes they support. This feature increases their influence beyond their dollar contributions. Large private foundations are the entities that were targeted in the California legislation discussed in the introduction, and we need to understand them in order to appreciate their significance to America's future.

---

* The exact percentage of total not-for-profit budgets provided by private foundations is difficult to determine, but it is clearly below 10 percent. The primary sources of funding for not-for-profits are federal and state governments and fees for service. A not-for-profit hospital, for instance, will derive income from charging fees for its services, with a portion of these fees paid by government entities such as Medicare.

*What Is a Private Foundation?**

A private foundation is a legally chartered entity created to provide funding to benefit the charitable purpose or purposes designated by its creator(s). These charitable purposes might include a single entity such as a museum or theater, a single cause such as animal welfare or early childhood education, a group of individuals (scholars or medical researchers, for instance), or perhaps a combination of socially useful activities. Such a foundation can be created either during the lifetime of the donor or by means of a bequest. Some foundations operate their own programs to provide such benefits (operating foundations) and others make grants to independent organizations, institutions, or individuals to carry out this work.

Private foundations differ from what are sometimes referred to as public foundations. Public foundations receive funds from many sources. The American Red Cross is an example of a public foundation. So too are the United Jewish Appeal, the Catholic Campaign for Human Development, and many others.

Private foundations are generally created by individuals, or groups such as families, to perpetuate (and manage) their philanthropic giving over time. Such individuals or groups have sufficient assets to provide their foundation with a lump sum of funds at the time of its inception, thus creating a corpus or endowment that can support the charitable

---

* There is a complex array of vehicles available today for the management of private philanthropy, including split-interest trusts and support organizations. These arrangements are not discussed here.

purpose(s). The corpus may be supplemented by additional gifts as the donor(s) see fit. The corpus is invested and expected to grow annually from prudent oversight by the foundation trustees.

Private foundations are state-chartered entities subject to the laws of the state in which they are created. To be chartered or incorporated, foundations must satisfy the state's requirements for a formal organizational structure and bylaws, which include: a statement of purpose, basic accountability and audit provisions, provisions for amending the bylaws, provisions for dissolving the entity, and the like. Governance requires a board of trustees who assume the fiduciary and legal obligations for prudent management—in compliance with state laws and in keeping with the wishes of the donor(s). The creator of a private foundation is entitled to select the initial trustees to govern the foundation (and to appoint himself if he chooses). As trustees need to be replaced, the remaining trustees select their new members.

Olivia Sage, who created the first general-purpose foundation in 1907 with a $10 million gift, appreciated the importance of the trustees in carrying out her intentions, and appointed three prominent women friends with lifelong experience in philanthropy (a radical departure from accepted practice), in addition to four distinguished men and herself. Once established, a foundation becomes the owner of any donated assets and a donor no longer exercises direct control over them. This means, for instance, that the majority vote of the trustees on any issue is final, even if the founder/trustee disagrees. In larger foundations, the trustees in turn hire professional staff to manage the work of the foundation.

Funds contributed to a private foundation with charitable intent receive favorable tax treatment at both the federal and state levels. At the federal level, the donor may deduct the gift, subject to a 30 percent adjusted gross income limitation. The activities of private foundations are also subject to a variety of spending rules and reporting requirements both at the federal and state level. These will be reviewed in chapter six.

Private foundations have the potential to exist in perpetuity, if the donor so wishes. In such a case, the trustees would invest the corpus and manage the funding of grants in such a way as to ensure the continued perpetuation of the fund itself. This exemption from the rule against perpetuities is a unique feature of the private foundation, enabling the donor to designate uses of the gift according to his or her wishes for all time.[1] This application of the perpetuity concept is different from the idea that Jefferson objected to. A foundation established in perpetuity is precisely designated to serve the greater good as identified in its donor intent and mission statements. It does not serve the personal interests of its donor or family in perpetuity as the British landed gentry experienced the perpetual benefit of land left to them. Donor freedom will assure that some foundations will spend down and others will grow to address changing needs over centuries. Diversity does matter.

Conversely, a donor may choose to limit the term of the foundation to a fixed period of time, and direct the trustees either to spend down the endowment within this time frame or to distribute the endowment in lump sums once the term is reached. George Peabody and Julius Rosenwald, for instance, both limited the terms of their foundations. At the end of the fixed term, the trustees distributed the remaining funds as designated by the donors and closed the foundations.

The corporate-like structure of foundations dates to the creation of the earliest single-purpose private foundations by businessmen familiar with such a framework. This was the way that Peabody, Slater, and others managed their for-profit activities. The regulation of limited and perpetual foundations is examined in chapter six.

Community Foundations and Donor-Advised Funds

While the majority of private foundations have been created by individuals and families, it is important to recognize two additional kinds of foundations. Community foundations are just what they sound like: organizations that collect, manage, and administer funds from individuals that are usually devoted to support for a given town, city, or geographic region. However, these funds are not pooled, but held as separate trusts or endowments within the framework of the community foundation.

Individual donors thus enjoy many of the benefits of establishing a private foundation. They can detail their wishes for ongoing donations from their fund. They can enjoy recognition for their giving through named funds and involve their family members in deciding on categories of needs they wish to address in their communities. Donors also avoid the financial costs of managing a separate endowment and the legal complexities of operating an independent private foundation. Community foundations number over seven hundred across the nation today, a number that continues to grow.

The donor-advised fund (DAF) originated within community foundations. In this case, a donor can make a lump-sum donation to the fund (technically a public foundation) and receive an immediate tax benefit. To be eligible for such a benefit, he or she gives up formal control of these funds. The trustees of the DAF control the funds and invest them according to their own investment policies. These trustees agree in advance, however, to provide gifts from the original donation to charities specified by the original donor. The popularity of these vehicles has grown exponentially in the past two decades, aided in part by the establishment of donor-advised foundations by retail brokerage/money management firms such as Fidelity, Vanguard, and Schwab. In 2008, for instance, these three companies took in some $3 billion in donor-advised fund contributions.

The Size and Scope of the Private Foundation Universe
At present, some 75,000 grant-making entities in the United States make funds available for the greater good. Private foundations account for about 90 percent of this total. In recent years, the number of foundations and the value of their collective assets have expanded exponentially. As of 2008, these entities held $670 billion in assets. This number represents roughly a 100 percent increase over the past decade. Foundation giving

has expanded as well, tripling over the decade 1997 to 2007 to some $42 billion. Such rapid growth, not surprisingly, has coincided with a period of expanding personal wealth, especially for the upper 10 percent of the income spectrum. This total of $42 billion represents approximately 12 percent of the $306 billion given by American citizens in 2008.

The assets of private foundations are not evenly distributed. Some 60 percent of all private foundations have assets below one million dollars. The largest private foundation, the aforementioned Bill and Melinda Gates Foundation, had assets in excess of $39 billion at the end of 2007. Over sixty foundations have assets in excess of $1 billion, according to the latest Foundation Center data.[2]

Another important metric for foundations is their giving per year. Once again the Foundation Center provides the data, ranking the top one hundred foundations by their total giving on an annual basis. As might be expected, there is a close correlation between the two listings, although there are exceptions. For instance, the Susan Buffett Foundation ranks number six in total giving, but number eighteen in total assets. Likewise, the T. Boone Pickens Foundation ranks twenty-ninth in total giving in 2008, but does not appear within the top one hundred foundations by assets. This particular giving list also features a significant number of corporate foundations, all in the health-care field.

Twenty-four community foundations number among the four hundred largest recipients of donations in the United States in 2008. While one might expect these large and successful community foundations to be based in major U.S. cities, a small number are located in midsized American cities such as Tulsa, Oklahoma, and Columbus, Ohio.[3]

What Causes Do Private Foundations Support?

Our American system of philanthropy provides foundation donors with a seemingly infinite array of organizations and causes that they can support. There are close to two million not-for-profit entities chartered in the United States today. The Giving USA Foundation is itself a 501(c)(3) organization devoted to the documentation of American philanthropic activity. It collects and aggregates data on private foundation giving by theme or target area on an annual basis.* In recent years, the areas of education (25 percent of total giving) and health (20 percent of total giving) have received the largest proportions of foundation support. The next largest categories are human services and public affairs/society benefit, the latter a category that includes giving to federated organizations, such as United Way, United Jewish Federation, and all free-standing donor-advised funds. These categories each account for approximately 16 percent of contributions by foundations.

The question of where foundations focus their giving, both today and in the past, is central to the issues that concern us here, given the data published by the Greenlining Institute and NCRP. The brief snapshot of activity offered here

---

* Of course, the definitions of the categories are important for understanding the data. So too the decisions of assigning programs. Education includes all levels, from pre-school through graduate. But does a grant to support art in the schools get assigned to education or to the arts?

is designed to fill in a section of our capsule portrait of private foundations. We will look more closely at the historical patterns of foundation giving in chapter five. For now, in the competition for philanthropic dollars, it appears that health care, education, and environmental causes have experienced the fastest growth in recent years.[4]

The Geography of Private Foundations

Private foundations were originally concentrated in the northeastern U.S., in keeping with the early population centers of the nation. In recent decades, however, there has been a balancing of foundation geographic distribution. Looking again at the top one hundred private foundations by asset size, we find that eighteen operate in California, twenty in New York, and seven in Texas. In all, fifteen states are represented among the top one hundred. Taking a slightly different view, 50 percent of foundation assets are based in six states: New York, California, New Jersey, Washington, Texas, and Illinois.* These statistics affirm that major foundations operate in all four geographical regions of the country.

Why Do Wealthy Individuals Create Foundations?

I have already proposed my own answer to this question. Wealthy Americans create foundations because they are generous. They are doing what the Founding Fathers hoped and believed citizens in our democracy would do. They are helping to

---

* This issue of geography is important because regulation of private foundations begins at the state level.

deliver on the promises of the Declaration for all citizens. But we also have more detailed information[5] on the motivation of donors who choose to create a private foundation, rather than using some other mechanism for their charitable giving.

Wealthy donors (and legal advisors) were queried by researchers in the 1980s about reasons for establishing a foundation. Most said they preferred to make decisions themselves (i.e., through their trustees) about how their fortunes would be spent to help others rather than to turn the funds over to the government in the form of taxes. Fully three-quarters of legal advisors queried felt that control of the assets was a prime motivation of foundation creators, with this wish obviously connected to the question of taxation. Many donors expressed a desire to take control of solving problems at the citizen level, rather than relying on government programs. The second reason for foundation establishment concerned the systematic features of such an entity. Donors expressed a desire to plan and manage their giving with intention, rather than simply responding to requests for support.[6]

This latter reason was often connected to a family or religious tradition of giving, as well as a sense of gratitude and responsibility for the careful stewardship of accumulated wealth. Twenty years later, there is additional research that updates these findings. Paul Schervish points out, for instance, that in recent years more wealthy parents have expressed worries about the negative impact of inherited wealth on the lives of their children and grandchildren.[7] With these worries has come a tendency to limit the size of inheritances and to establish private foundations as a convenient way to manage the situation. Schervish has coined the phrase "the new physics of philanthropy" to describe this and other recent trends he has identified in his extensive research on wealthy givers.

For instance, he notes that there has been an exponential increase in the number of young people with great wealth, often of their own making. These individuals achieve (and recognize) their financial security at earlier ages than has historically been the case. Rather than concentrate on adding to their personal wealth, they are turning their entrepreneurial skills and energies to hands-on philanthropy. They have the assets to establish foundations and the desire to make a systematic, long-term commitment to the greater good. Schervish cites an essay by John Maynard Keynes entitled "Economic Possibilities for Our Grandchildren," written in 1930. At the start of the Great Depression, Keynes speculated that the "economic problem" —i.e., achieving sufficient wealth to be financially secure—could well be solved for many Americans within a century. He predicted that this would change the "nature of one's duty to one's neighbor. For it will remain reasonable to be economically purposive for others after it has ceased to be reasonable for oneself."[8] What a wonderful thing if we were just beginning to glimpse this phenomenon at its earliest stages!

How Do Private Foundations Do Their Work?

The trustees are responsible for determining the goals and strategies deployed by a private foundation. In the case of larger foundations, a president or executive director, responsible to the trustees, carries out the executive functions for the organization. Such basic management functions as the preparation of an annual operating plan, a budget, and a year-end report documenting activities are universal elements of foundation operation dating back to the creation of the first foundations. It is also common to organize staff into program-focused areas that reflect the interests and priorities of the foundation. The Russell Sage Foundation—established by Olivia Sage in 1907—eventually organized a set of program areas that included child hygiene, industrial studies, statistics, recreation, and survey and exhibits, among others. This structure enabled the development of expertise among staff members, and in this case, inaugurated the social-scientific approach to the needs of society.

At a high level, private foundations generally play one of three roles in the projects they undertake:[9] they act as leaders (drivers) of the initiative; they act as partners in moving the initiative forward working with other organizations (other foundations or not-for-profits, or perhaps government or private entities); or they act as catalysts, meaning that they focus on funding the work of others, offering a limited amount of input or guidance. This last approach is the most familiar—when a foundation responds positively to a request for funding from a not-for-profit organization, expecting an annual report on how the funds have been spent in compliance with the funded proposal. The foundation may well have an interest in the field where the not-for-profit is working, but it does not play an active role in the implementation of the funded work.

Partnerships have become more common in recent years as larger private foundations have established expertise and interest in specific problem areas. They may work on project development with recipient organizations—revising plans as new information comes to light and adding to their expertise in the process—but they recognize that they have neither the expertise nor the resources to drive the effort independently. Joel Fleishman offers examples of foundations investing in academic disciplines as examples of partnerships, such as Rockefeller's support for molecular biology, or the Olin Foundation's investments in law and economics. He also describes so-called venture philanthropy as a variant of the partnership model.[10]

Finally, there are dramatic examples of foundations, often larger ones, with the resources to initiate change efforts, lead the thinking, hire the expertise directly, pay the bills, and persevere as needed to reach the intended goal. Such was the role played by the Robert Wood Johnson Foundation in the establishment of our national emergency response network, the 911 system. Similarly, the Carnegie Corporation spearheaded the drive to create the Corporation for Public Broadcasting.

What Are the Tangible Benefits of Private Foundation Work?

Foundations provide support to a wide range of beneficial activities in keeping with the diverse interests of their creators.

They do so mostly through contributions to those two million organizations designated as not-for-profit by the federal government. The government is extremely generous with such designations, enabling entities ranging from medical research institutions and universities to community theaters and community garden associations to receive foundation support. Their purposes are broadly categorized into the following thematic groupings: health, religion, education, human services, arts and culture, environment and animals, and public affairs/society benefit.

It is evident that this burgeoning marketplace of ideas has proved a winning arrangement for all concerned. Taxpayers, as represented by the government, enjoy economic and social benefits from foundation efforts that greatly surpass the value of taxes not collected by the government because of the tax exemptions offered. The study cited in chapter one found an economic gain of $8.58 for every dollar invested by private foundations.[11] The $42 billion in grants in 2007 thus created some $368 billion in total direct economic value. Even taking into account the possibility that these figures are inflated, as I noted earlier, there is a clear economic advantage to the incentive approach. The greatest benefits, however, are less tangible.

Intangible Benefits

It is wonderful to have economists who are able to quantify the value of investments and the benefits that accrue. I think we can agree, however, that the dollar figures greatly undervalue the importance of philanthropy in general and of private foundations in particular. We recognize intuitively that the value of a college scholarship for a deserving but financially needy student cannot be captured by the dollar value of the scholarship. It cannot even be estimated by calculating the difference between total expected lifetime earnings of high school graduates and of college graduates.

The value of the investment must be measured in terms of the intangible: the increased self-esteem and optimism of the recipient, the potential positive influence this individual may exercise on family and friends over a lifetime. And how to measure the benefits that all of us may realize from the work this individual accomplishes because of education and training? Moreover, I anticipate that this individual will become another champion of generosity stemming from his or her gratitude for the opportunity of the scholarship, further multiplying the value of the initial investment.

Investments by private foundations have also enabled change at the system level. Lives have been enhanced—not simply one at a time, but for millions of citizens—through improvements in public health, public safety, and the quality of our environment.

Foundations as Learning Organizations

The work of private foundations offers an additional, ancillary benefit to society. A donor or donors create a foundation to ensure the sustained support of one or more beneficial activities. If sustaining the work is not a priority, a one-time gift will do just fine and an institutional structure is not required. But a commitment over years—and in some cases, decades— enables a foundation to develop valuable knowledge about a given issue, about what works and what does not work and perhaps even why this is the case.

We associate Andrew Carnegie with one of the great philanthropic efforts in our nation's history: the building of public libraries in cities and towns across the nation. Carnegie's father brought his family to America from Scotland in 1848 when Andrew was twelve. He grew up outside Pittsburgh, and often recalled happy memories of time spent in the reading room his father had established for the use of his workers. Over his lifetime, Carnegie built and then sold the United States Steel Company. Beginning in the 1890s, Carnegie, without the aid of a foundation structure, began building libraries in the communities where his steel mills were located, presumably to encourage his workers to take up the challenges of self-improvement. As word spread of Carnegie's willingness to fund such projects, inquiries came in from many additional towns and cities. Carnegie and his secretary, James Bertram, formulated a set of guidelines for dealing with these requests. To be eligible for support, a municipality would be required to provide a prime building site for the facility and to commit to spending a sum equal to 10 percent of the Carnegie gift from its own resources each year for maintenance, operating expenses, and book purchases.

By 1911, Carnegie had spent some $30 million of his own money on these projects, and he elected to establish a foundation called the Carnegie Corporation to continue this as well as his other charitable work. The corporation invested an additional $13 million in the library construction program, eventually accounting for the building of 1,679 libraries across the nation. (Carnegie funded an additional nine hundred libraries outside the United States during this period as well.)

Carnegie was driven by a powerful and idealistic vision that all citizens should have access to the accumulated knowledge of the ages. Self-discipline and self-improvement would carry the nation forward. Carnegie's idealism was tempered, however, by his pragmatic business experience and his understanding of human behavior. If a community was not willing to invest *with* him in creating and sustaining this community asset, he was not willing to invest.

His vision and his strategy created leverage that advanced the quality of life in many communities beyond his grant-making. Citizens seldom required public officials to put library creation at the top of a town's priority list in the decades before the Carnegie program. Subsequently, however, even towns that did not receive support from Carnegie began to build libraries in order to enhance the desirability of their communities for residents and businesses.

The Carnegie trustees wished to study the impact of the library building program. A consultant was hired (even in those days!) to analyze the successes and failures and to report candidly to the board on the program. The consultant found many elements that were sub-optimal and recommended improvements. His report noted, for instance, that there was a shortage of qualified librarians to run the libraries effectively and that the foundation should shift some resources to the professional education of library staff. The trustees were apparently not very happy with these findings (even in those days!), so they chose instead to terminate the library-building program. Eventually, the foundation did support a number of the recommendations, but not in a way that saved the building of libraries as a priority.

What matters for our purposes, however, is the role that the foundation can naturally play in assessing its own investments in (social) change efforts. Created for sustained effort, a properly managed foundation can develop the longitudinal data and institutional memory necessary to evaluate its own impact. Such learning as would naturally take place through sustained effort could be captured, analyzed, and recycled for the benefit of the foundation itself and other interested parties.

The I Have a Dream program has likewise used its foundation as the core knowledge-management resource for a network of local initiatives. In 1981, Eugene Lang spontaneously offered to pay $2,000 toward the college tuition of each student in the class of sixth graders he was addressing at PS 121 in East Harlem, New York. Lang was the immigrant son of Hungarian refugees when he had attended this very same school some forty years earlier. He was working in a restaurant to support his family with few thoughts of college. But a chance encounter with a trustee of Swarthmore College encouraged young Gene to pursue his love of learning. He went on to a most successful career as an entrepreneur, building and selling several manufacturing companies.

His impulsive act of generosity spawned a privately funded network of "Dreamer" support programs in cities across America. Like Carnegie, he initially funded his program on the fly, paying for tutorial and counseling services for the first group of students as he learned what it would take to move these at-risk students to a level where they could take advantage of his initial pledge. Five years later, in 1986, he established the I Have a Dream Foundation to ensure the sustained funding of his vision. Today, the foundation guides a network of thirty-one affiliate chapters, supporting over 3,500 kids from families below the poverty line, having already helped over 11,000 poor kids reach for the goal of post–secondary education, this among a population where more than 50 percent drop out before completing high school and fewer than 15 percent obtain a bachelor's degree.[12]

Lang's foundation has accumulated a deep understanding of best practices and elements of success to guide local start-up programs. It is able to share this critical knowledge with idealistic but inexperienced local funders and entrepreneurs. In so doing, the foundation contributes to program efficiency gains and builds the human-capital resources of the nation. Such recycling of accumulated wisdom, especially in the domain of social experimentation, is all too rare. While private foundations are far from perfect at such practices, they do offer, as these stories illustrate, opportunities for creating smarter social policy. I intend to provide additional stories as we dig deeper into the synergy between American foundations, our market-based economy, and our representative democracy. But we should now turn to a more detailed analysis of this delicate balance.

Each gift is part of a system of reciprocity in which the honor of giver and recipient is involved.

–Mary Douglas,
"No Free Gifts"

CHAPTER FIVE

Private Foundations: A Brief History[1]

The mindset of the entrepreneur is an essential asset of American prosperity: Peter Cooper, Cyrus McCormick, and Carnegie in the nineteenth century, and Larry Ellison, Steve Jobs, and Michael Bloomberg in the twentieth have all displayed remarkable vision and pursued their visions with determination and persistence. They articulated their ideas in such a way that others were willing to share in the risk of inventing the future by investing in their projects. They also possessed the ability to transform their visions into reality. They were astute planners and risk managers, pragmatic decision-makers, and shrewd investors in both people and ideas. Their optimism and independence define the mindset that has enabled America to grow and to prosper, despite wars, financial panics, and epidemics.[2]

Our social-profit sector has grown and prospered for the same reasons: the relentless commitment of citizens to a better future for all citizens. I like to think of all participants in the virtuous cycle as seekers of social profit. We want to increase the goodwill and mutual concern that unite us as a people. This profit is not a responsibility of government. It must be produced by citizens, and it is a special responsibility of individuals with the means and the gifts to lead these efforts. Such individual initiative on behalf of the greater good is the competitive advantage that has enabled us to welcome millions of immigrants to our shores and to build a cohesive, productive, and prosperous society.

Private foundations have proved to be a vital force in the pursuit of social profit. A small number of successful men (and women heiresses) put their accumulated fortunes to work in pursuit of this goal in the late nineteenth and early twentieth centuries. They brought their sense of determination and self-discipline to their philanthropy through the foundation structure. They could set priorities, evaluate opportunities for philanthropic investment, communicate with petitioners, document their activities, and engage their trusted colleagues (through positions as trustees) in their problem-solving efforts. While some have theorized that private foundations arose as a kind of default mechanism to compensate for the lack of government leadership, it seems more appropriate to see this development as an extension of a long tradition of citizen commitment to community building. The foundation provided a structure to deal with larger problems

and larger sums in an efficient way. The female social entrepreneurs of America's nineteenth century—lacking great
fortunes, but not lacking in commitment or entrepreneurial
skills when it came to serving their fellow citizens—had developed their own collective structures to support and fund
their efforts. These associations, with the women's exchanges
providing the most advanced example, reflected their members' idealism, intelligent planning, and personal caring in the
service of their fellow citizens.

This historical overview concentrates on *what* private
foundations have done for the nation over the past one hundred years. It is a surprising and remarkable story of innovation
and leadership. These stories will, I hope, elicit a "Wow, I didn't
know that!" response. We are all beneficiaries of citizen generosity through private foundations, every day, and often we are
simply not aware of what we should be grateful for. When we
consider that private foundation giving has always constituted
a relatively small percentage of funds available to support the
greater good, the impact of these investments is nothing short
of remarkable. I hope you will share my pride and enthusiasm
when you read these too-good-to-be-true stories.

> Charity in its legal sense comprises four principal
> divisions: trusts for relief of poverty, trusts for the
> advancement of education, trusts for the advance-
> ment of religion, and trusts for other purposes
> beneficial to the community, not falling under any
> of the preceding heads. . . . *The trusts last referred*

to are not the less charitable in the eye of the law, because incidentally they benefit the rich as well as the poor, as indeed every charity that deserves the name must do either directly or indirectly.[3]

This quotation from Lord Macnaghten of England in 1891 provides a framework for the history of the American foundation. In the nineteenth century, in America as well as in England, much charity focused on assisting those in need of basic assistance such as food and shelter (the poor), on spreading the Christian religion, and on support for more universal education. But Lord Macnaghten adds an all-important additional category to charity. He includes *any* other activity that will benefit the community. In so doing, he opens the door to the imagination of the philanthropist and the entrepreneur and removes the constraints of a traditional focus on poverty, religion, and education. He also makes an additional point that is highly relevant to our discussion. It is not necessary that philanthropic activity serve *only* the poor or unfortunate in order to qualify as charitable. On the contrary, all effective philanthropy serves the interests of the community of citizens, which includes the giver as well as the recipient.

The first private foundations in America, as I noted in chapter one, emphasized the importance of providing education to all. Early philanthropists understood the fundamental lessons learned by the colonists, that everyone in the "newe land" would benefit when each and every able member of society was educated to the highest level of his capacity. In modern terms, the nation could not afford to waste any human capital. An officer of Yale University defined this uniquely American ideal in 1831:

> The College is also in want of funds for the relief of necessitous students. Individuals of this class have not infrequently risen to the highest stations of influence and authority in the nation. The welfare of our republic requires that such men be educated. Other colleges very generally offer education to them at reduced price. Yale must therefore do the same, both to promote the interest of the community and to secure her own prosperity.[4]

This is the essence of "self-interest, rightly understood."

The First Private Foundations

George Peabody launched his Peabody Education Fund in 1867 for the purpose of promoting "intellectual, moral, and industrial education in the most destitute portion of the Southern States." His fund is regularly cited as the first private foundation in America, and it was soon followed by the Slater Fund, designated for the purpose of "uplifting the lately emancipated population of the Southern states, and their posterity, by conferring on them the blessings of a Christian education."

A history of private foundations in America should begin, however, with the following passage from Benjamin Franklin's will from 1789:

> The said sum of one thousand pounds sterling, if accepted by the inhabitants of the town of Boston . . . is to be let out the same at interest of five per-cent, per annum, to such young married artificers under the age of twenty-five years, with good moral character. . . . [T]hese loans are intended to assist young married artificers in setting up their business. . . . It is hoped that no part of the money will at any time be dead, or diverted to other purposes, but be continually augmenting by the interest. . . . [T]herefore there may in time be more in the loan fund than the occasion in Boston shall require, and then some may be spared to the neighboring or other towns.*

Franklin proposed a perpetual revolving loan fund, rather than a formal foundation, a kind of venture capital fund. He did not appoint trustees, but trusted to the city fathers to pursue his donor intent. The idea of providing a lump sum

---

* Cited in David Blankenhorn, *Thrift: A Cyclopedia* (West Conshohocken, PA: Templeton Press, 2007), 104. Franklin made a similar gift to the city of Philadelphia and even computed the balance of the funds after one hundred and again after two hundred years and how they should be distributed on these anniversaries. For what happened, see Walter Isaacson, *Benjamin Franklin: An American Life* (New York: Simon and Schuster, 2003), 474–75.

for the perpetual support of a worthy cause (Franklin clearly saw civic benefits from the encouragement of entrepreneurs) began with the Founding Fathers.

But back to the Gilded Age and the modern private foundation. When Caroline Phelps Stokes died in 1909, she bequeathed $800,000 to a fund to be used to build housing "for the poor families of New York City and for educational purposes in the education of Negroes both in Africa and the United States, North American Indians, and needy and deserving white students." Phelps Stokes was a pious and well-educated woman who had traveled extensively throughout her life with her older sister, Olivia. She was well informed about the needs of these marginalized groups. Her trustees, guided by Thomas Jones (who directed the fund from 1913 until 1946), invested in scholarships and in research on the needs of Africans (the Phelps Stokes family was instrumental in establishing and supporting the country of Liberia) and of American Indians. The United Negro College Fund and the American Indian Educational Fund, both the largest philanthropies of their kind today, trace their lineage directly to investments from the Phelps Stokes Fund.

These examples of early, single-purpose private foundations underscore the American commitment to education for all and to citizens as the prime movers in addressing social needs well in advance of the government. The work of Franklin, Peabody, Slater, and Phelps Stokes also illustrates two additional defining characteristics of American generosity. These philanthropists gave well beyond their own frameworks, recognizing the needs of others who were far removed from their daily lives. Empathy and awareness of the needs of others at a time of relatively little information flow testifies to a kind of generosity driven by a vision of larger needs than the world outside one's front door. This view also implies a willingness to give across geographical boundaries, another feature of our philanthropy. Generosity within and among families and communities has its precedents in virtually every society, but few demonstrate such extraordinary giving across racial, ethnic, and geographic boundaries in pursuit of a greater good for all.*

The General-Purpose Foundation

The first general-purpose private foundation was the Russell Sage Foundation, created with a $10 million transfer from her inherited funds by Olivia Sage, Russell's widow. The date was April 1907. The mandate was unique and far reaching: "the improvement of the social and living conditions in the United States of America." The approach to this challenge, as specified in the inaugural charter, was likewise multifaceted: "to use any means for that end . . . including research, publication, education, the establishment and maintenance of charitable or benevolent activities, agencies and institutions." Olivia's

---

* Edmund Burke appreciated this unique feature of American social development. He wrote that "we begin our public affections in our families . . . we pass on to our neighbourhoods." He used the term "little platoons" to describe the immediate group we belong to and saw it as a necessary first step toward eventual love of country and mankind. See *Reflections on the Revolution in France* (London: J. M. Dent and Sons, 1955), 44.

plan (strongly influenced by her attorney, Robert DeForest) was followed quickly by Rockefeller and by Carnegie, each of whom established broader, general-purpose structures for their philanthropy within the next five years.

These philanthropists were part of a remarkable generation of wealthy citizens. In 1870, there were about one hundred millionaires in America. By 1916, there were some 40,000. The size of their fortunes was impressive as well. Olivia Sage had become the wealthiest woman in America when her husband died in 1906, leaving her a $75 million fortune (roughly $1.5 billion in today's dollars). This sum was dwarfed by the $400 million Carnegie had earned when he sold U.S. Steel in 1901. Rockefeller's fortune was greater still.

While the great majority of the wealthy were not particularly generous, and those who were generally confined themselves to giving at the local level, the small number of very generous, very bold-thinking philanthropists had a disproportionate impact on the development of the nation. These individuals included Olivia Sage, John Rockefeller and his son John D., Jr., Andrew Carnegie, Julius Rosenwald, Edward Filene, Edward Harkness, and Elizabeth Milbank, each of whom established a general-purpose foundation at the beginning of the twentieth century.*

---

* The work of each of these individuals merits a volume of its own. The department store magnate, Filene, for instance, used his personal fortune to champion the creation of credit unions in Massachusetts in order to enable working people to borrow for emergencies at reasonable rates, rather than falling victim to loan sharks. He was an exemplary steward of his fortune for the greater good as well as an embodiment of the idea of "self-interest, rightly understood." See Roy Bergengren, *Credit Union North America* (New York: Southern Publishers, 1940), 94.

In varying degrees, they pursued ambitious agendas that sought to change the nation at the systems level. Others could build a local hospital to care for the sick, but the big thinkers would not be satisfied until the diseases that afflicted the citizens were cured. Rosenwald called it "wholesale philanthropy," in keeping with his profession as a retailer (he was part owner of Sears, Roebuck and served as CEO from 1908–24). Better to leave individual giving to individual citizens, he said. Foundations should take on change at the system-wide level. Rosenwald personally took on the building of an entire network of elementary and secondary schools and community centers for blacks across the rural south. By the end, he had cofounded 5,327 such schools. It was the mindset of the entrepreneur, of a successful man who had rethought and reconfigured the systems of commerce and sought to apply the same bold vision and risk-taking mentality to social problems. He also insisted on matching investments from each community where he established a school.

An overview of these heady times for private philanthropy should give top billing to Olivia Sage. She was seventy-eight years old when her husband died. Russell Sage had been famous for his good fortune in speculative businesses, his taste for gambling and other earthly pleasures, and his lack of generosity. Olivia, up to this time, had acted the role of a benevolent Victorian lady, making small charitable gifts to worthy causes serving the less fortunate. She was pious and concerned about her position in New York society as the wife of a "nouveau-riche" husband (in comparison to, say, the Astors).

Chapter Five

When her wealth became known, she was inundated with requests for money from needy individuals and institutions, as well as those who sought funds for new projects and new ideas. She created her foundation at the suggestion of Robert DeForest, her husband's attorney and himself the longtime president of the Charity Organization Society (COS) in New York, which functioned as the first professional society for charities. In fact, COS infrastructure was used to assist Olivia in the management of her giving before the establishment of her foundation.*

The Russell Sage Foundation embraced a progressive agenda—what came to be known as scientific philanthropy. The foundation funded the first effort to document the scope and shape of urban poverty in America. The Pittsburgh Survey produced six reports, beginning in 1909, that detailed the economic, social, and health conditions of working women, steel workers, mill workers, and other wage earners. The study proved highly influential, shaping policy efforts for decades to come. The staff of the foundation, among the nation's first sociologists, went on to influence the efforts of social reformers and policymakers right through the

---

* Olivia Sage, having given only a percentage of her wealth to her foundation, continued an active personal philanthropy throughout her remaining years, focusing on the needs of women, on animal welfare, on higher education, and on civic philanthropy. (She tried and ultimately failed to inspire the community of Sag Harbor, New York, where she had a summer home, to adopt a progressive community development agenda with her support. DeForest was the developer of Forest Hills, now a section of Queens, New York, using an innovative public-private funding structure—what we would call today a "blended solution.") See Ruth Crocker, *Mrs. Russell Sage* (Bloomington: Indiana University Press, 2006).

New Deal. The foundation established the casework model of social services. When funders such as Sage, Rockefeller, and Carnegie paid to support positions in these emerging fields at the University of Chicago, Harvard, and Columbia, the knowledge-based, data-driven approach to social science became institutionalized.

The various Rockefeller foundations, guided strongly by Robert Gates, championed this systematic approach to social problem solving at the root-cause level. While there were plenty of social Darwinists at the time who felt that only the strongest and most adaptable among the needy would and should prosper, Rockefeller, Sage, and others felt that such law-of-the-jungle thinking was abhorrent when it came to human communities. Gates and Rockefeller, both Baptists who espoused an engaged form of Calvinism, believed that they had a duty to raise all God's children to a higher level, so that all would be able to prosper.

The other major focus of the large private foundations in the early years of the twentieth century was scientific and medical research. Support for such work continued to expand in the years following World War I. They were intent on strengthening the nation for its expanded leadership role in the world. Rockefeller (1901) and Carnegie (1902) developed and funded their own institutes (later universities) devoted to science and technology, and they supported many others.

Foundations made large-scale investments in research universities, both private (Cornell, Duke, Western Reserve, and Northwestern, as well as Yale, Harvard, and Princeton) and public (the universities of California, Michigan, Wisconsin, and Texas). All poured funds into science for the public good. Remarkable public-health advances emerged from this private-funding campaign to attack diseases from a scientific standpoint. Hookworm and other "filth" diseases were greatly reduced, thanks to public-health campaigns funded by the Rockefeller Foundation and based, for their intervention techniques, on research into disease patterns supported with private dollars. Carnegie supported the first research that led to the successful extraction and refinement of insulin for the treatment of diabetes. Rockefeller enabled the development of the first antibiotic, penicillin, through funding to Howard Flory and Boris Chain, who were able to isolate and purify the active ingredient in the *penicillium* mold discovered by Alexander Fleming a decade earlier. This development paved the way for large-scale production—just in time for the onset of World War II.

In the 1930s, in yet another example of high-risk investment in intellectual capital during a time of many competing needs, the Rockefeller trustees determined to invest in the emerging field of experimental biology. Under the leadership of Warren Weaver, the natural-sciences division funded a wide range of research projects encouraging collaboration among biologists and physical scientists (physicists, chemists, and the like). The outgrowth of this work defined modern molecular biology, beginning with the Krebs cycle within cells and culminating in the discovery of the structure of DNA by Watson and Crick.[5] It is worth noting as well that the federal government spent no money on scientific research until the 1950s, when Congress approved the first institute of health under enormous pressure from, you guessed it, a private foundation, in this case the Lasker Foundation, led by Mary Lasker.

Private foundations also took an interest in an area that, like basic science, would ultimately define our modern nation. In this case, the area was national defense, and the story is another of those "only in America" tales of risk and transformative success. This foundation project foreshadowed a sustained and complex effort over much of the twentieth century that involved private foundations in national-security issues.

When a young World War I flyer named Harry Guggenheim returned from Europe, he was in love with airplanes. His vision was nothing short of utopian:

> Airplanes are the harbingers of peace, the instrumentality that will bring about a lasting sympathy among nations . . . [and] close communication between various communities. . . . The airplane will bind nations together through increased understanding.[6]

Harry went to work on his father, Daniel Guggenheim, a highly successful mining and smelting magnate who was following in the footsteps of his own father, Meyer. By 1925, Harry had persuaded his father to make his first investments in this new technology of flight by funding a school of aviation at New York University. Daniel went farther and eventually persuaded Calvin Coolidge to make the federal government a partner in the effort. Coolidge directed some $3 million of government support to the Guggenheim Fund for the Promotion of Aviation.

Meanwhile, America's aviation hero, Charles "Lucky" Lindbergh, whose 1927 solo transatlantic flight had galvanized the nation, sought out Daniel Guggenheim to make the case that aviation had a future that went far beyond airplanes. He spoke of the experiments of a young physicist, Robert Goddard, who had built and launched successfully a solid fuel rocket in 1929. Even the exploration of outer space would soon be technically possible. Over the next decade, Guggenheim invested well over $1.2 million in Goddard and his work. He also funded schools of aeronautical engineering at MIT, Caltech, Stanford, Harvard, Georgia Tech, Syracuse, and the universities of Michigan and Washington. These early investments paved the way for developments as profound as instrumental flying, and ultimately, the American space program. The jet propulsion laboratories at Princeton and Caltech were funded by Daniel through the family foundation in the 1950s, along with endowed professorships named for Robert Goddard.

The Guggenheims also understood the importance of advocacy. They mounted an aggressive campaign to promote commercial aviation, hiring Lindbergh and other pilots to barnstorm the nation, visiting fairs and engaging the public's imagination. While the government was an early, if cautious, partner, it took the drive and vision of a truly entrepreneurial family to lead the nation into a new era of national-security technology and commercial development. Astoundingly, there is a similar story to tell about the development of another technology that also became a cornerstone of American security: radar. The private philanthropist who made it possible is Alfred Loomis.*

By the time of the stock-market crash in 1929, there were about 180 private foundations in the nation, hardly a huge number. But the crash had many consequences for private-foundation philanthropy.[7] It soon became evident that even the largest foundations could not meet the burden created by the collapse of the economy. Up to this point, most citizens believed that support for those in need should come from the community (churches, the community chest, fraternal groups, auxiliaries). Foundations were also confident in their ability to research and deliver social services through support to an increasingly sophisticated network of social-service providers. Herbert Hoover had proclaimed in 1930 that the citizenry could and would, he was confident, care for their fellow citizens in need as the economy collapsed. He had appointed a panel of prominent citizens to coordinate the all-volunteer effort. But all were soon obliged to look to the newly elected Franklin D. Roosevelt and the federal government to lead the way out of the Great Depression. And thus, for the first time, dozens of charitable organizations came to rely, in whole or

---

* Loomis was a wealthy lawyer/investor who survived the crash of 1929 with his fortune intact. He turned his mansion in Tuxedo Park, New York, into a salon/laboratory for the greatest scientists of the era between the wars. I tell this story in detail in *The Greater Good* (New York: Henry Holt, 2003), 115–16.

in part, on "grants" from the government to support their work on behalf of those in need.*

Private foundations contributed as well, of course, but many rightly continued their support, even in such difficult times, for cultural institutions and for new ideas. The Duke Endowment funded the experiments in health-care financing that led eventually to the creation of Blue Cross and Blue Shield in the mid-1930s in North Carolina. Alfred Cowles, a stockbroker deeply troubled by the crash and his own inability to predict market movements, created a foundation to explore the connections between mathematics and economics. Over the years, the Cowles Foundation sponsored the work of nine Nobel laureates, including Harry Markowitz, James Tobin, Kenneth Arrow, Lawrence Klein, and Paul Samuelson. Cowles-sponsored scholars created the first stockmarket index and invented the field of econometrics. Henry Ford launched Greenfield Village (before establishing his foundation) to celebrate the accomplishments of American inventors and entrepreneurs. John D. Rockefeller III poured millions into Colonial Williamsburg and enduring American institutions such as the Museum of Modern Art in New York City (built on Rockefeller-donated land).

World War II presented a vast set of challenges to America's private foundations. On the heels of the investments in

---

* With the government's involvement in the traditional fields of charity have come opportunities for cooperation with private philanthropy, as well as potential conflicts, over the past seventy-five years. I will say more about the growth of the welfare state and the challenge it presents to private foundations in chapters nine and ten.

medicine and technology that had prepared the nation to face yet another global conflict, there now emerged a new set of demands. Should charity dollars be used to ransom those held captive by fascist regimes? Such payments were authorized by charitable traditions dating to the Renaissance,[8] but it was unclear how such payments could be effectively deployed. Many millions of dollars were channeled to provide education to Jews excluded from access by Nazi regimes in Poland and elsewhere in the 1930s. Perhaps the most fruitful investments created havens for those fortunate enough to escape the Nazi onslaught, including Albert Einstein and John von Neumann, who found a home at the Institute for Advanced Studies at Princeton, which had been funded by a $5 million gift from Louis Bamberger and his sister, Caroline.

The post–World War II era was dominated in many ways by the Cold War, and private foundations played an active role in the defense of American ideals. Carnegie, Mellon, Ford, and Rockefeller (among others) took up the challenge and invested heavily in agricultural and economic development programs in South Asia, East Asia, and Latin America. The same was true in Africa, where each regime change on that fragile continent became a contest between the world's two great superpowers. The so-called development decade was underway. Rockefeller supported the University Development Program, designed to strengthen African universities. Ford supported the National Institute of Political Studies in the Congo (as well as population studies), and Carnegie launched the Africa Liaison Committee to coordinate teacher-training efforts.[9]

When the Communist empire collapsed, private foundations once again stepped in to assist the nations of Eastern
Europe with the challenges of transition to a free society.
Since the 1970s, the Soros Foundation and its allied Open
Society Institute Network have supported dissidents and promoted free-enterprise and democratic institutions through an
unprecedented network of some sixty private foundations
around the world. George Soros, a refugee from Hungary and
a successful currency trader, created this highly decentralized
model. It continues to donate hundreds of millions of dollars
annually across all of Eastern Europe and the former Soviet
republics.[10] Ronald Lauder, one of the heirs to the Lauder
cosmetics fortune, likewise took up the task of rebuilding the
Jewish communities of Eastern Europe shattered by the Na-
zis and the USSR. The Lauder Foundation has created educational and religious training programs for young people in
over a dozen countries.[11]

The end of World War II also brought many changes
in American domestic life. One of the greatest accomplishments of the era was the G.I. Bill, which created access to
post–secondary education for millions of Americans who
might otherwise have never considered the possibility. Private foundations took up the challenge of helping to manage this educational revolution. Ford and Carnegie created
the National Merit Scholarship program, and a decade later
Carnegie sponsored the development of national measures
of educational progress. The Scholastic Aptitude Test was
born.

Education remains an area of continuing creativity for private foundations to this day. As our national attention has shifted repeatedly between the need for better preschool education and the need for improved secondary education, particularly in urban areas, foundations have produced and funded some of the most inventive and high-impact initiatives of our era. *Sesame Street*, the defining early educational experience of two generations of American children, was created through the combined efforts of the Carnegie and, later, the Ford foundations. Whatever one may think of Kermit and Miss Piggy, the work of the Children's Television Workshop and Joan Ganz Cooney constituted a great leap forward from Howdy Doody (with all due respects as a former fan)!

The work of the Bradley Foundation offers another illustration of educational innovation. In the 1970s and 1980s, there emerged a great deal of troubling data about the educational progress of children in poor urban neighborhoods. These concerns had sparked the idea for *Sesame Street*, for the federal Head Start program, and other initiatives. The Lynde and Harry Bradley Foundation—based in Milwaukee, Wisconsin, and newly enhanced by assets from the sale of the Allen Bradley Co.—launched a campaign to test an idea of the free-market economist Milton Friedman. Why not allow parents to shop for the best school for their children, using vouchers representing the public cost of educating their child in the neighborhood school?

The foundation funded the initial research and policy papers to build support for a pilot program that, once underway, was stopped by the Wisconsin courts in response to a lawsuit filed by the state superintendent of public instruction. Bradley undertook the funding of a voucher pilot on a private basis, investing $1.5 million to enable poor kids to attend private and parochial schools of their choice. A few years later, Bradley gave $20 million to enable private schools in Milwaukee to expand in order to accommodate more voucher kids. Many more millions from Bradley, and also from the Joyce Foundation, went to pay the costs of litigation at the state level. Eventually, in 1998, the state Supreme Court upheld the voucher legislation passed years earlier, enabling public voucher education to proceed. By this time, many thousands of Milwaukee kids had been educated through the programs funded by Bradley and many businesses in the region. The U.S. Supreme Court upheld the voucher program in 2002.

Meanwhile, a complementary movement, the creation of charter schools, was initiated in the early 1990s with support from the Walton Foundation, established by the family that founded the Wal-Mart chain of retail stores. Here the idea was to create new schools within the public-school framework—smaller, more flexible, and often theme-based—in order to multiply the number of learning environments available to children. Many foundations supported this work, and today charter schools are a growing part of the educational landscape, with over 3,500 in operation across the nation.

Finally, I want to provide a concluding story that I hope will clinch my argument that private foundations have pioneered the creation of important—and often unrecognized—

features of modern life. In 1952, John Dorr of Westport, Connecticut, wrote to the state highway commissioner urging him to consider painting a white line on the outside edge of the traffic lanes on the Merritt Parkway. Dorr offered to pay for the project himself. Dorr was a retired metallurgical engineer who had built a very successful company and created a private foundation in 1940. The foundation was chartered to support Dorr's favorite fields of chemistry and metallurgy, as well as special education for kids and other worthy causes.

But he became interested in traffic safety in that era of two-lane highways at the urging of his wife, who complained that bright oncoming headlights caused her (and others) to steer away from the center line almost involuntarily. Dorr hypothesized that a white stripe on the outer edge of the pavement would guide drivers in staying on the pavement even when they looked away from those approaching headlamps.

The Connecticut authorities agreed to a test and the results suggested a significant reduction in accidents when compared to historical accident rates in the areas where the outside stripes were added. Soon the entire Merritt Parkway was striped. New York undertook its own test on the Hutchinson River Parkway, again with positive results. However, due to increased traffic patrols during the testing period, critics argued that the test was flawed. Many other states found reason to object to the idea as well, from the cost (estimated to be $150/mile) to the danger that motorists would mistake the white stripe for the center line of the road—with disastrous results! The Dorr Foundation countered with an initiative to fund extensive independent testing in four additional states, designed and monitored by the National Highway Safety Board.

The results again favored Dorr's idea, and local media coverage gradually turned public opinion in its favor. Today, in an era of divided highways and precision-focused Xenon headlamps, we take the white stripe for granted as part of the American landscape—an unlikely but highly valued gift to all of us from private philanthropy.

The Private-Foundation Landscape Today

In 1987, the Council on Foundations and the Yale University Program on Non-Profit Organizations (PONPO) published a set of essays entitled *America's Wealthy and the Future of Foundations*.[12] The studies examined the diminishing popularity of private-foundation creation in the wake of the 1969 Tax Reform Act. The authors surveyed thousands of wealthy individuals and concluded that the government policy did have a significant impact on foundation creation. Given the reporting and spending requirements initiated in the late 1960s, only the wealthiest citizens could see the merits in creating a private foundation to manage their philanthropic activities. For the majority of wealthy individuals, donor-advised funds, community foundations, and direct contributions provided a sufficient system for generosity. At the time, the Ford Foundation was America's largest private foundation, with assets two to three times greater than the next largest foundation, Kellogg.

The academic researchers did not foresee the impending surge in wealth creation that emerged in the next decades through a combination of financial engineering, technological innovation, and advantageous tax policies. During the 1990s, a new era of biotechnology and telecommunications created fortunes on a scale last seen in the Gilded Age one hundred years earlier. The creation of private foundations once again assumed an upward trajectory at an exponential pace. It peaked in the year 2000 with the creation of some 6,400 private foundations in that single year. In 2009, the Foundation Center counted more than 75,000 grant-making entities in the U.S.

Asset accumulation likewise reached levels that would have been difficult to predict two decades earlier. In 2007, private foundations' assets reached close to $700 billion, although, as we all know, this number fell back by approximately 25 percent during the downturn of 2008, only to reassume an upward trajectory during 2009. Once again, the landscape was dominated by a single foundation, although it was no longer Ford.

Giving by all private foundations has likewise kept pace, reaching as high as $45 billion by some estimates in 2007. Private foundations are active today across the widest possible range of social, scientific, and cultural concerns, still investing in human, physical, and intellectual capital for the benefit of the nation. While many foundations have sustained their traditional focus on improving health-care delivery, technology, education, and the arts, there has been an increase in investments in policy studies and other research work designed to validate, or invalidate, various approaches to government policy. This work, which has often taken on an overtly political resonance, has led to a proliferation of think tanks with various colorations across the political spectrum. I will return to this phenomenon in the next chapter on government regulation of foundation activities.

A second theme of contemporary foundation concern is often described by the term globalization. As the world has shrunk through airline travel and telecommunications, the contingencies of modern life have become more evident. Everyone is aware as never before of the impact of our own actions on others—and of their actions on us. We are impacted by agricultural practices in Latin America (burning of rainforests), by sanitation practices in Africa (infectious diseases), and by manufacturing practices in Asia (mineral prices, emissions). Private foundations have led efforts to understand our environmental interdependencies (the Goldman Foundation, the David and Lucile Packard Foundation, Betty and Gordon Moore Foundation, John T. and Catherine A. MacArthur Foundation, and many others), as well as our health/disease/technology interdependencies (Gates, Markle) and our energy interdependencies (Hewlett, Sloan).

Finally, Paul Schervish has noted the increase in wealth accumulation by an ever more diverse and younger group of citizens. I want to point out the remarkable number of private foundations created by these individuals, whether they have made their early fortunes as successful money managers, athletes, Web entrepreneurs, or entertainers. Our tradition of generosity is certainly alive and well on the contemporary scene among these talented people. From Geraldo Rivera to Russell Simmons, from Angelina Jolie to Dolly Parton, from Sergey Brin to Dikembe Mutombo, the list goes on and on. In fact, I would wager that a majority of professional athletes in the United States today have created private foundations. The multifaceted world of contemporary entertainers has embraced the private foundation as a vehicle to support a variety of causes as diverse as their creators.

It is important to note, of course, that the majority of private foundations are not created by the ultra-rich and famous. Among the 75,000 private foundations, about half are family foundations. About 60 percent of these have assets under $1 million.[13] In fact, only about 6,000 private foundations employ staff to direct their activities. American generosity has always extended beyond the ultra-rich. Over the past one hundred years, a special kind of foundation has grown alongside the other private foundations: the community foundation. This vehicle has provided smaller donors with many of the advantages of a professional foundation infrastructure: staff, investment management, reporting requirements, and the like. The key is the word "community."

History of Community Foundations

The first community foundation was created in Cleveland, Ohio, in 1914. Frederick Goff—a lawyer, influential citizen, and president of the Cleveland Trust Company—is credited with the idea, inspired by a combination of civic-mindedness and business efficiency. Cleveland Trust managed many small trusts, and Goff proposed that they be grouped together and their administration undertaken by an entity other than the bank. Cleveland Trust would stick to doing what it did best: managing the money.

But Goff's vision was much greater than the creation of a new bit of bureaucracy. He envisioned that such an entity could over time build up a "great fund" for the well-being of the city of Cleveland, what he called a "community chest." He envisioned that the enterprise would encourage local generosity and in turn provide leadership for the city's needs. He hoped to avoid the problems that had plagued the bank in administering the small trusts. He told *Collier's* magazine:

> What if a man making a will could go to a permanently enduring organization—what Chief Justice Marshall called an "artificial immortal being" —and say: "here is a large sum of money, I want to leave it to be used for the good of the community, but I have no way of knowing what will be the greatest need of the community fifty years from now, or even ten years from now. Therefore, I place it in your hands, because you will be here, you and your successors, through the years, to determine what should be done with this sum to make it most useful for people of each succeeding generation.[14]

Goff's idea was a great success, and the Cleveland Foundation today has about $1.5 billion in assets. Over its long life, it has made over $1 billion in grants to the community it serves, thanks to the generosity of Cleveland citizens. The idea spread rapidly to other cities. Within a few years, New York, Boston, and Chicago had established their own "community chests." Today, there are over seven hundred community foundations nationwide, an increase of 100 percent in the past two decades. Particular credit for this expansion is due to the Lilly Endowment, based in Indianapolis. Lilly sponsored the creation of community foundations in each of the counties of the state of Indiana through its GIFT (Giving Indiana Funds for Tomorrow) program. These Indiana community foundations today control assets in excess of $1 billion, up from $100 million in 1990. Nationally, community foundations manage some $30 billion in assets, and make some $2 billion in grants annually. There is even a rapidly expanding international network of community foundations, numbering about three hundred.[15] The largest of the American community foundations, the New York Community Trust, manages in excess of $2 billion in assets.

Community foundations still generally serve a local purpose. Leaders like Emmett Carson have led community foundations (Minneapolis and Silicon Valley) and have also helped to further refine the public role of these special foundation entities. As Carson said in an interview with the *Stanford Social Innovation Review* in 2007, "If you're not interested in an institution that's active on community violence or what's happening to immigrants, you probably aren't going to be at a community foundation."[16] Donors to community foundations often feel local loyalties and many fulfill important roles as advocates for the needs of the neediest. At their best, community foundations help to advance their communities by connecting committed grassroots leaders with the imaginative ideas of their funders.

Community foundations provide an efficient mechanism for local citizens to give money to the communities they love. In the 1980s and early 1990s, when many local community hospitals were purchased by for-profit health-care companies, the proceeds from these sales frequently went to community foundations and strengthened their financial reach. Today, many community foundations also operate within their structure another innovation in private philanthropy—the donor-advised fund.

History of Donor-Advised Funds[17]

Donor-advised funds (DAFs) originated within the framework of community foundations. The first such fund was created in the early 1930s, perhaps at the Winston-Salem Community Foundation in North Carolina. Interest in such vehicles was modest until the 1980s and gained momentum throughout the 1990s. Assets in such funds reached $28 billion by 2007, up from $7.5 billion at the turn of the millennium.[18] While community foundations continue to offer such funds, much of the growth has been driven by the efforts of major retail money-management firms. Vanguard, Fidelity, and Schwab alone have some $7 billion under management. A small number of colleges and universities have also established donor-advised funds (Harvard and Cornell among them). Finally, a number of organizations have been created in recent years that specialize in the management of DAFs: Donors Trust, the National Philanthropic Trust, and the Foundation of Philanthropic Funds, to name but a few of the larger ones. The National Philanthropic Trust, for instance, currently manages about $750 million in such funds, providing a wide choice of investment managers and educational services concerning philanthropy to its clients. These entities do a brisk business today in converting small family foundations into donor-advised funds. Given the nature of DAFs, the profile of their contributions matches the full spectrum of giving preferences among generous Americans.

Has charity become all law?
Is it irrecoverably committed to lawyers
instead of its traditional practitioners?

–Robert Goheen

CHAPTER SIX

Private Foundations and Government Regulation[1]

The issue of government regulation begins, of course, with the fundamental question of public trust. The extent to which the government takes an interest in regulating institutions and legal entities is directly correlated with their actions. Any behavior that raises questions about trustworthiness invites inquiry and potential regulation. This brief history examines this relationship of trust over the past century. As we will see, foundations have often been buffeted by opposing forces, particularly during periods of increasing income disparity between rich and poor. Populist legislators have worked from the impulse to treat private foundations with suspicion. These legislators have regularly asked for more transparency and more accountability. On the other side, defenders of private foundations have pointed to their good works and their important contributions to social, cultural, and scientific advances. They have argued that the value of these obvious accomplishments outweighs any lack of transparency and adhered generally to the view that if it isn't broken, don't fix it.

Private foundations enjoyed considerable public support as they grew in numbers and prominence at the beginning of the twentieth century. The virtuous nature of the undertaking, the dispensing of one's private funds to support public purposes, seemed to all concerned the very definition of virtuous behavior of a citizen in a democracy. The views of Andrew Carnegie on the responsibilities of the man of wealth, as set forth in his *Gospel of Wealth*, were widely praised, and the need for regulation seemed slight.*

The government acted accordingly in the early years of the twentieth century. The first federal interest in the regulation of private foundations occurred in the period 1912–15. The U.S. Commission on Industrial Relations (the Walsh Commission) was created by an act of Congress to look into labor/management issues at a time of increasing conflict between corporations and their unionized workers. The commission spent considerable time looking into the Rockefeller industrial empire and also at the role of the family's various foundations that had been created over the preceding decade.†

---

* See the Carnegie quotation that begins on page fifty-five.

† The inquiry was certainly influenced by the disastrous massacre of twenty strikers and family members, including employees of the Rockefeller-owned Colorado Fuel and Iron Company, by Colorado National Guardsmen in Ludlow, Colorado, in 1914.

While the work of the Walsh Commission in the area of philanthropy had little immediate legislative impact, the recommendations made concerning private foundations were remarkably contemporary in feel. They included the idea that foundations with over $1 million in assets (a major foundation at the time) should require a federal charter and that the accumulation of funds in such foundations should be limited, as should the amount of their expenditures. The commission further recommended that foundations report periodically on their activities to the government, and, in a sign of the times, the commissioners went so far as to recommend that the government itself should step up funding in such areas as education and social services in order to counter the pervasive influence of private foundations.

None of this came to pass, but the issues had been placed on the table. The War Reform Act of 1917 put in place for the first time a federal personal income tax and recognized religious, educational, scientific, and charitable organizations as exempt from taxation on income. The idea of providing a deduction for charitable contributions was also introduced at this time.[2] This provision, which established an incentive for charitable giving, has been a cornerstone of our federal and state tax policies ever since.* The act left the chartering of foundations to the state level while ensuring that such entities

---

* Given the progressive nature of the U.S. personal income-tax system, the benefit of a deduction is greater for an individual in a higher tax bracket (a higher-income earner) than for a lower-income worker. For a spirited criticism of this policy, and many useful bibliographical references, see Rob Reich, "A Failure of Philanthropy," *Stanford Social Innovation Review* (Winter 2005): 24–33.

would also be exempted from various state taxes (property, estate, sales, and so on).

Actual regulation of foundations was by and large very relaxed. The charitable deduction was hardly a driver of charitable giving over the next several decades, as it benefitted only a very small percentage of citizens. Wealthy individuals seldom created foundations for purposes of tax avoidance. There were, nevertheless, opportunities to use these vehicles to personal advantage. For instance, some companies donated all their assets to foundations and then leased them back, thus avoiding business taxes. This was the mechanism that permitted the Ford Motor Company to pass to Henry Ford's descendents without taxes upon his death. A special class of voting stock went to the descendents, and a new class of non-voting stock was contributed to the foundation, thus freeing the estate of any tax liability. When the non-voting stock was sold on the open market, it made Ford the richest foundation in the nation.

Between 1917 and 1950, nothing much changed for foundations from a regulatory perspective. Even with the great expansion of federal programs during the New Deal, no formal legal distinctions were made between funders such as foundations and service-provider organizations. Separate regulations were first introduced in tax legislation in 1954, but only formalized in detail in the Tax Reform Act of 1969.

In 1954, however, another problematic practice attracted the attention of Congress. Charities had begun to

take ownership of for-profit entities that had no relationship
to their missions. They used these feeder operations to produce income and treated the income as tax-exempt. One of
the most famous cases is New York University Law School's
ownership of the Muller Macaroni Company, America's largest pasta maker during the 1940s. In 1954, Congress passed
the Unrelated Business Income Tax (UBIT), which required
charities owning income-producing businesses to pay taxes
on the business profits.[3]

Also in the early 1950s, foundations encountered a form
of government review that was more ideological than regulatory. Despite their firm capitalist roots, foundations did not
escape the scrutiny of zealous anti-Communist legislators.
Even John D. Rockefeller III was compelled to testify about
the expenditures of the Rockefeller Foundation and to defend
its support of such controversial activities as the research of
Albert McKinsey on human sexual behavior (a clear threat to
decency and morality, according to Rockefeller's inquisitor).
The Cox Committee, and later the Reese Committee, eventually agreed that foundations seemed free of direct Communist sympathies. However, the committees noted the lack of
public accountability of these foundation entities. A requirement was adopted that foundations file annual reports with
the IRS, although many were quite reluctant to do so.

The 1960s were a turning point in the relationship of the
federal government and private foundations. Representative
Wright Patman of Texas began a crusade for greater federal
oversight of foundations. His campaign lasted throughout

the turbulent decade. Foundations were again on the defensive and once again the Rockefeller family took the lead in pushing back. The criticisms offered by Patman are familiar: a lack of accountability and transparency in the use of private foundation funds despite the fact that they have been "subsidized" by the citizenry through the tax code. Patman argued that foundations were exploited by the wealthy, especially in matters of corporate control. Pete Peterson, then the CEO of Bell and Howell, was candid in his testimony to the Senate Finance Committee:

> . . . the most attractive feature of the use of a foundation is that it enables the donor, at least in some measure, to have his cake and eat it too. He obtains a tax deduction at the time he makes a donation to the foundation; yet he can still exercise a substantial measure of control over the assets which he has donated to the foundation. The point is, of course, of particular importance when the asset contributed . . . is stock in family controlled or otherwise closely held business.[4]

It was clear to John D. Rockefeller III that foundations could not afford to do nothing in the face of Patman's crusade. He urged the Treasury Department to take a more active interest in auditing the practices of foundations. He suggested that the Treasury issue a set of guidelines: a prohibition on self-dealing, denial of tax deductions for property donated to closely held foundations, shortening of terms of board members, and the like. The Treasury accommodated.

The Revenue Act of 1964 did not seriously impact private foundations, despite the efforts of Patman. But Rockefeller made a very public effort to address the question of trust in private foundations. He called for "taking stock" now that foundations had a fifty-year history. He argued that philanthropy was not addressing society's "new and unmet needs," and proposed that "we should be prepared to think of government as a partner in those areas where it shares the burden of support."[5]

Rockefeller recognized that self-regulation among foundations would be an important and visible step to restore confidence. He organized a commission of widely respected leaders from government, academe, and business—chaired by the above-mentioned Pete Peterson—to explore self-policing mechanisms for private foundations and ideally to get ahead of the populist tide that saw Wilbur Mills, chair of the House Ways and Means Committee, talking about a 20 percent tax on foundations. Peterson and his work group identified many issues that are familiar in foundation critiques today. They included a lack of innovation, an occasional lack of generosity, and a tendency to bureaucratic inertia. Peterson himself came out strongly in favor of expanded IRS audits of private foundations and the creation of a quasi-governmental oversight board for all charity organizations. He did not, however, endorse a proposal from Senator Albert Gore that the life of all private foundations be capped at a forty-year maximum.

None of these more radical ideas were included in the next tax-reform act that passed Congress in 1969. There were, however, several provisions in the legislation that regulated private foundations in new ways: a required 6 percent annual payout rule and a 4 percent tax on endowment income. (These requirements have subsequently been amended and are now set at 5 percent and 2 percent respectively.) The act also formally differentiated charities for the first time, with separate rules for public charities (501[c][3]s), private foundations (grant-makers), and operating foundations (essentially not-for-profit businesses). It also included limitations on ownership of controlling blocks of corporate stock by foundations and less favorable tax treatment of assets contributed to foundations compared to contributions to public charities.

A bitter pill, perhaps, but few considered the legislation a disaster for private foundations. The greatest impact was to drive numerous small private foundations to contribute their assets to local community foundations and to cease operating as separate entities. Perhaps there was a lesson in the fact that the Peterson Commission issued a formal report only *after* the tax-reform legislation had been enacted (about as exciting as last year's fashion forecast, said one wag). Needless to say, Peterson's determined efforts to bring together a plan for self-regulation by the foundation community proved fruitless.

Against the backdrop of the war in Vietnam, these regulatory concerns about private foundations carried little urgency. Implementation was slow as well, as the IRS struggled to clarify the new rules. In the early 1970s, Rockefeller once again felt that an effort was needed to dig into the relationship of private philanthropy and tax policy and to work for clarification of key foundation concerns, especially the matter of what precisely constituted the line between advocacy (permitted) and lobbying (not permitted).[6]

A new group of business and academic leaders was assembled—headed by John Filer, CEO of Hartford Insurance—and an ambitious agenda of research projects developed. The group was accorded 501(c)(3) status. It commissioned numerous (ninety-one!) studies of the impact of tax policy on corporate giving, the dimensions of the issue of tax avoidance through foundation creation, and other fundamental questions.

Once again, however, events in Washington overshadowed the work of a Rockefeller-supported commission on philanthropy. Watergate, the resignation of Vice President Spiro Agnew, and eventually of President Richard Nixon occupied the headlines. Commissioners also struggled to reach a consensus on the policy implications of their extensive research. The final report of the Filer Commission, "Giving in America," satisfied few commissioners and was filled with dissenting comments (a freelance writer was hired to write it over a few months' time). In fact, we can trace the positions at odds in the world of private philanthropy today directly to the views expressed at the conclusion of the Filer Commission deliberations.

Some members felt that the report was too defensive about philanthropy and that core ideas were distorted:

Another defect in the report is the distortion of
the concepts of "equity" and "democracy" applied
to philanthropy by the "wealthy." The fact that the
wealthy make the largest gifts and have the freedom
to decide the object of their gifts is referred to as
inequitable and undemocratic. . . . Givers should
be able to designate the purposes and objects of
their gifts.[7]

Others felt sufficiently strongly to insist on filing a dissenting report, which they prepared with the support of Rockefeller and Filer. Entitled "Private Philanthropy: Vital and Innovative or Passive and Irrelevant," the Donnee Group, as
the dissenters were dubbed, focused on constituencies rather
than on philanthropists. They highlighted the increasing needs
of the poor, the women's movement, and minorities. As they
put it in their report:

We regret that the Commission too often failed
to recognize that it was dealing with public policy
issues affecting the lives of real people. Regardless of how the pie is sliced, there is no question
that grants made directly for social change or to
assist the powerless are dwarfed by the massive
philanthropic contributions made annually in support of education, the arts, health services, and
the like.

The report continued with a comment from the women commissioners: "Philanthropy can only fulfill its role in American society if it is willing to listen to the advocates of social change, that is, those who are articulating public needs from the point of view of those in need."[8]

Despite Rockefeller's heroic effort to partner with the government and to embrace dissent, the words of Commissioner Leon Sullivan summed up the state of things in 1975 as the commission wrapped up its work: "There is a preponderant view in America that a large majority of the foundations are not sensitive to the basic gut concerns of the country."[*]

The Donnee Group morphed in a short time into the National Committee for Responsive Philanthropy (the same NCRP discussed in this book's introduction). The *Wall Street Journal* noted that the commission report brought to light a difference in giving patterns between the wealthy and the not-so-wealthy, with the former favoring education, hospitals, and the arts, and the latter favoring religion. It also noted that charitable tax policy had a much greater impact (read: benefit) on the wealthy, given the graduated income-tax structure.

---

[*] Eleanor Brilliant, *Private Charity and Public Inquiry* (Bloomington: Indiana University Press), 111. Sullivan, a Philadelphia minister and developer of the Opportunities Industrialization Centers (OIC) in the 1960s, is perhaps best known as the developer of the Sullivan Principles to guide international corporate behavior in relationship to the apartheid government of South Africa. In the 1960s, he raised considerable private funds to launch the OIC idea before attracting government support. See Leon Sullivan, "From Protest to Progress: The Lessons of the OIC," *Yale Law and Public Policy Review* 4, no. 2 (1986): 364–74.

A final brief point on the Filer Commission recommendations. The report recommended that restrictions on lobbying activities by not-for-profits (501[c][3] designees), imposed by the 1964 tax law, be loosened, but these recommendations did not apply to private foundations.*

Rockefeller was killed in a car crash in 1978, and the era of Rockefeller-sponsored commissions ended. There was a sharp decline in the creation of new private foundations during the 1980s, although total giving by all individuals did not reflect a similar drop-off. Theresa Odendahl provides ample documentation that the various reporting and spending regulations contained in the 1969 Tax Reform Act had a negative impact on the number of private foundations created during this period. This downturn did not last very long and was perhaps due, in retrospect, to a variety of factors, from the upheavals of the oil embargoes to the growing interest on the part of financial advisors in split-interest trusts and other philanthropic vehicles. As noted above, the growth rate picked up again exponentially as the technology revolution took hold in the 1990s.

The struggles over issues of transparency and accountability were not resolved to anyone's satisfaction in the ensuing years. Private foundations are chartered as state-level entities, not federal ones. As a result, a complex and overlapping set of regulations and guidelines govern charity law.[9] Much of

---

* In a famous case, the Sierra Club had its 501(c)(3) designation revoked by the IRS because of lobbying activities in 1966. Supporters complained bitterly that the IRS covered up for exempt organizations found to be supporting the CIA and did not impose the same fate.

this patchwork, ironically, is the result of efforts to bring some measure of uniformity to the myriad state laws governing charities. The Uniform Management of Institutional Funds Act (UMIFA) was agreed upon in 1972 by the Uniform Law Commission and eventually adopted by forty-seven states. (It was updated in 2006 and is now called the Uniform Prudent Management of Institutional Funds Act [UPMIFA].) States are still in the process of adopting the new, recommended laws, although by the end of 2008, some forty-three states had already signed on.

As the name suggests, these new recommendations focus mainly on spend rules for charities with respect to their invested funds, clarifying the definition of income, and firming up guidelines for prudent management in cases where endowments have fallen below certain levels.[10]

In 2006, as part of the Pension Protection Act, Congress enacted another round of regulatory actions affecting private foundations. The changes were primarily technical in nature, and far too numerous to review here. There is little doubt, however, that they continued to add to the reporting requirement for both donors and foundation managers.[11]

In conclusion, it seems fair to say that the level of trust between the elected representatives of the citizenry and private foundations has remained in flux since the delivery of the Filer Commission report in the mid-1970s. This trust issue clearly dates back to the 1960s, and the commission report documents a tension that had already been building in America for well over a decade. The effort to develop a plan for self-regulation among foundations proposed by Rockefeller and others has yet to come to fruition.

However, the partnership between private foundations and the government that Rockefeller envisioned has occurred more often, at least on the programmatic level. Recent American history is full of projects in which the initial investments by private foundations have demonstrated workable ideas that the government has subsequently taken to scale. The right-hand, reflective white line on U.S. highways was such an initiative. Charter schools, school vouchers, the Corporation for Public Broadcasting, and dozens of other efforts have followed this model.* The Obama administration is initiating a social innovation project in search of good foundation ideas that could form the bases for new private foundation/ government partnerships.

The foundation world of today is large and growing. There is little evidence that the growth of regulation (and the attendant managerial complexity) has dampened the enthusiasm of Americans for the establishment of private foundations. This unique American institution has proved popular with Americans of virtually every racial and ethnic background. These include African-American donors like Eddie and Sylvia Brown giving in education, arts, and culture;

---

* Of course this role for government also reflects the resources available. Irving Kristol famously accused large private foundations of the sin of pride in pursuing large-scale, systemic change projects that they could not fund. He argued that foundations would be more effective if they stuck to "creating good individual schools" rather than seeking to "reform education." See Leslie Lenkowsky, "Irving Kristol's Legacy for Philanthropy," *Chronicle of Philanthropy*, September 21, 2009.

Bill and Camille Cosby, whose foundation focuses on health; Earvin "Magic" Johnson, who is working on economic development; Will and Jada Pinkett-Smith, who specialize in foster care and adoption; and John Rogers, Alphonse Fletcher, and Oprah Winfrey, among many others.

Asian-American philanthropists are represented by Chinese-American Leslie Tang Shilling, a generous donor both to Chinese needs and to more general projects in the U.S. (including a $4 million gift to MIT). George Aratani, Japanese-American founder of Mikasa and Kenwood Electronics, was interned as a young boy and has given over $10 million to a range of causes. The ranks of Hispanic-American donors are growing rapidly as well. Foundations like Robert Goizueta's provide funds for education. Danny Villanueva, Sr., not only gives generously, but teaches philanthropy to Latinos. Villanueva established Destino: The Hispanic Legacy Fund, dedicated to creating philanthropic and leadership opportunities for Latinos in California's Ventura County. The fund, created in 1996, was Villanueva's attempt to include previously excluded Hispanic families in the philanthropy process. Native-American Mike Roberts, a member of the Tlingit tribe, does the same work as president of First Nations Development Institute. Roberts is currently launching fifty-four foundations in tribes working with him.

The rich tapestry of philanthropy includes Americans of all ethnicities and is a tribute to the solidarity we feel as voluntary citizen donors. I do not believe that more laws could make this diverse philanthropy better, richer, or more

varied than it is. The good works freely undertaken by generations of donors inspire current citizens' philanthropic activity
as a way of expressing their freedom. It is a tribute to the
heirs of enslaved blacks and of Native Americans that they
choose to engage in philanthropy despite the difficult history
their ancestors survived. A level of government interest and
oversight is inevitable, given the scope of private foundation
activity. Despite the tangled and tedious regulatory environment, however, the basic elements of our dynamic private
philanthropic system remain. The IRS charitable deduction
remains solidly in place, providing a gentle incentive to do the
right thing. Perhaps more importantly, this deduction symbol-
izes our government's embrace of America's marketplace of
private generosity.* So too does the policy that encourages the
creation of countless 501(c)(3) organizations to compete for
funding from generous citizens (and the government!).

But John Rockefeller's worries have hardly disappeared.
The work of trust-building must continue. We can only hope
that Robert Goheen's lament offered at the beginning of this
chapter does not become a reality on the fiscal side. In the
next chapter, I will take a look at an area of private philanthropy that many would agree is already dominated by the
legal profession.

---

* Suggestions by Congressman Becerra and others that assets held in private
foundations are somehow quasi-public because of the charitable deduction seem to
confuse incentives and subsidies. For a well-reasoned legal critique of this view, see
Evelyn Brody and John Tyler, "How Public Is Private Philanthropy? Separating Myth
from Reality" (monograph, Philanthropy Roundtable, 2009).

The earth belongs in usufruct to the living.
–Thomas Jefferson

*The day that philanthropists start believing
charities are under no legal obligation to adhere
to the terms of their gifts is the day many will stop
giving. That would be a tragedy for the millions of
Americans these charities help every years.*
–William Robertson

*At bottom, the problem of fidelity to the original
intent in both judging and foundation administration
is one of self-discipline in the service of the Founders',
rather than one's own, moral purposes.*
–Robert Bork

*[N]o wise man will bind trustees forever to certain
paths, causes or institutions.*
–Andrew Carnegie

CHAPTER SEVEN

The Importance of Donor Intent in Citizen Generosity[1]

The private foundation is a rare example in American law of an entity that can exist in perpetuity. The Founders were in general opposed to any arrangements in perpetuity. As noted earlier, this notion reminded them of the mechanisms by which European aristocrats had maintained family lands and fortunes for generations—to the disadvantage of the larger populace. Jefferson was particularly outspoken on the issue of perpetuity, writing to Madison in 1789 that "the dead have neither powers nor right over [the earth]." But there existed a large body of English law favoring the indefinite perpetuation of charitable—i.e., noncommercial—institutions, such as churches and universities, and the Founders chose to respect this tradition. They were much more concerned about preventing perpetual inheritance within families across the generations.

As we saw earlier, Benjamin Franklin clearly envisioned that the fund created in his will would continue for centuries. Other donors had different ideas about the merits of perpetuity. George Peabody and Julius Rosenwald chose to place time limits on their foundations. Olivia Sage, John Rockefeller, and Henry Ford did not. Neither did Andrew Carnegie. Donors thus differed not only about the terms of their foundations, but also about how their foundations should be managed after their deaths. Franklin took great pains to spell out exactly how he wished funds in two geographic locations to be dispensed over the centuries, while Carnegie explicitly gave his trustees great latitude to use their own judgments.

There may be little disagreement that donors should enjoy complete freedom when selecting the causes they wish to support, but there are clearly many opinions about *how* the giving should be done. As time passes and circumstances change, a host of nettlesome questions arise, and we should hardly be surprised that many cases end up in court (including Franklin's). Thus it is instructive to ask, in cases where conflict has arisen about the use of foundation resources, how have the issues been resolved and what reasoning has been applied? Once this background has been examined, I want to review the non-legal aspects of donor intent—from the point of view of the donor, of future generations of his or her family and trustees, and of society at large. If there is one lesson to be learned from history, it is a simple one. The more concerned a donor is about preserving his or her intent in perpetuity, the more preparation and careful work that donor must invest in advance of the creation of a private foundation.

The Legal Overview

The tension at the core of the debate, as expressed by legal historian Marion Fremont-Smith, is the following:

> . . . the potential clash between the desires of donors to control the disposition of assets they have given for charitable purposes and the needs of the public to assure that those assets are being used to meet current needs.[2]

It is difficult to make a broad generalization about the contemporary legal status of donor intent. Every case in the past several decades has turned on narrow points of law and varied according to the state in which the litigation was brought. Donor intent is established in the courts by the "instrument" or written document used to create a bequest or foundation.

In order to enjoy the tax benefits of a charitable gift, donors (or their estates) have been required to give up all direct control of their gifts when they create a foundation. They have had little legal recourse if they or their heirs are unhappy with the uses to which their gift is put by their trustees or by a recipient institution.* Only the state attorney general, representing

---

* Gifts to a community foundation are treated differently: "A community foundation's governing body retains variance power by which it may modify any restriction or condition on the distribution, if circumstances warrant." See http://www.cof.org, Standard II, Part E. The variance power is a distinguishing feature of

the citizens of the state, had legal standing to intervene in such circumstances.

If and when a gift could no longer be put to its intended use because the need no longer existed (when a disease, for instance, was cured), the English courts developed a principle called *cy pres*. The doctrine established that trustees (and/or the courts) were empowered to use the gift for other purposes that were as close as possible to the intent of the original giver, in light of contemporary needs. In general, the courts held, trustees who wished to alter the donor's intent to fit new and different needs were obliged to prove two things: first, that the donor had "general charitable intent" when making the original gift, and second, that the current conditions made adhering to the exact specifications of the donor's intent "impracticable" or "impossible to achieve."[3]

American courts developed a further notion to address changes in perpetual charitable funds. This action is called deviation, and it enables the courts to alter the means by which a charitable fund operates. Thus a donor-imposed restriction on *how* a fund is invested (say, only in war bonds) can be modified. Courts have also used deviation to alter terms deemed illegal, such as discriminatory requirements. (A prominent Maryland case involved a bequest for the construction of a nursing home "for whites only.")

a community foundation, making it distinct from a private foundation. The IRS requires that the trustees have such authority over all funds in the community foundation in order to classify the funds as part of the community foundation and therefore for the donor to receive the full tax-related benefits.

So how have these concepts been used in American courts in recent decades? First, there has been a willingness in some cases to allow donors (or more often, their successors) to have standing to bring suit when they believe that donor intent has been breached. Historically, as noted above, the beneficiary's interests are represented by the attorneys general of the states when they choose to take the case. The basic case is the *Carl J. Herzog Foundation v. the University of Bridgeport*. The foundation donated $250,000 to the university to support scholarships for medical education, which were used to fund a nursing program. When the nursing school closed, the university began using the funds for other purposes. The foundation sued to enforce the donor's intent. The Connecticut Supreme Court ultimately ruled that the donor did not have standing to sue. The court reinforced the notion that the state attorney general was responsible for enforcing the public interest in the use of the gift.[4]

Recent cases, however, have created additional flexibility in some venues when they can demonstrate a special interest.[5] For instance, a Texas lawsuit seeking to enforce the terms of a gift to the Metropolitan Opera for use in presenting "traditional opera" brought by the estate of the donor was allowed to proceed. In New York, a suit against St. Luke's-Roosevelt Hospital brought by the widow of a donor also moved forward, with the court concluding that the donor (or his family) was often in a better position than the attorney general to enforce gift intent. The court granted the widow and the attorney general coexistent standing.

In California, a private foundation sued the UCLA Foundation and the regents of the state's higher-education system on the grounds that the private foundation's gift to support a chair in cardiothoracic surgery was being applied to different uses. The regents counter-sued, arguing that only the state attorney general had the power to enforce the provisions. The appeals court ultimately determined that the agreement between the private foundation and the regents was contractual, meaning that the private foundation did have standing in the case. The court also ruled that the attorney general's power to enforce charitable agreements was not exclusive.[6]

Interpretations that view a gift agreement as a contract can be used to justify the standing of the donor to sue, as a contractual promisee. The argument goes that given the lack of funds for their operations, the states' attorneys general are failing in this duty, and they are unlikely to do better in the future. This view can certainly strengthen the hand of either the donor or the beneficiary, but there are potentially negative tax consequences for a donor pursuing this perspective.

The Uniform Management of Institutional Funds Act (UMIFA),* adopted in 1976, spells out that donors are permitted to release restrictions on gifts that they previously imposed,

---

* This act and its recent update, the Uniform Prudent Management of Institutional Funds Act (UPMIFA), are efforts to bring into alignment a set of best practices across the fifty states that charter foundations. Inevitably they deal with donor intent, although only in cases where there is ambiguity. For instance, the acts provide detailed guidelines about the treatment of such ambiguous instructions from a donor as "spend the income from my gift . . . etc." by defining income in such circumstances. See Susan Gary, Letter to the Editor, *Chronicle of Philanthropy,* October 15, 2009.

although they do not have a right to impose modifications or the standing to sue to enforce restrictions. Guidelines further recommend that donors be asked to provide input (if available) on any changes. Donors may also bring *cy pres* actions themselves, provided that they have not stipulated a reversion clause in their gift instrument, meaning that they have reserved the right to reclaim the gift under certain circumstances.

With respect to the recent modification of the original UMIFA guidelines, there have been changes in the rules guiding the release or modification of donor restrictions which also strengthen donor intent. Courts may still amend the terms of a gift in the event that the donor is not available to do so and the original purpose is no longer viable. However, under the new regulations, the rules of *cy pres* must be followed after an amendment of the original instructions, meaning that every reasonable effort must be made to use the liberated funds for purposes that are as close as possible to the previous intent.* Guidelines also clarify that the intent of the donor is defined by the original gift instrument, not what either the donor (if living) or the court thinks it may be at the time that modification is requested.

Several cases in point show that some courts continue to enforce donor protections: the Robertson family was able to recapture a portion of its original gift to Princeton's Woodrow Wilson School (plus legal fees) in an out-of-court settlement

---

* Small funds (below $25,000 and older than twenty years) can also be modified by a charity itself, again guided by *cy pres,* provided the charity notifies the attorney general of its intent and provides a sixty-day period for comment.

after years of litigation. In another case, Vanderbilt University determined to change the name of a campus dormitory, Confederate Memorial Hall, that had become part of the university when it took in Peabody College for Teachers in 1979 (remember George Peabody?). The dorm had originally been paid for many decades earlier through pledges from the Tennessee chapter of the United Daughters of the Confederacy, which sued to preserve the name. The United Daughters prevailed on appeal and the university dropped plans for the name change.

The Uniform Trust Code (UTC), another of the efforts to bring uniformity across states to the structure and management of trusts, notes that "if a charitable purpose becomes unlawful, impracticable, impossible to achieve, or *wasteful* (italics added), the court may apply *cy pres* to redirect the trust, in whole or in part, in a manner consistent with the settlor's charitable purposes." I have highlighted the newly added term to illustrate an apparent widening of the circumstances in which *cy pres* actions may be brought.

In the case that some believe led to the addition of the word wasteful to the UTC, Beryl Buck created the Buck Trust upon her death in 1975 to benefit the poor in Marin County, north of San Francisco. Mrs. Buck estimated her gift, in the form of her ownership share of the Belridge Oil Company, to be valued at approximately $10 million. The funds were to be managed by the San Francisco Foundation, a community foundation supporting several counties adjoining the city. In 1979, Belridge was sold to Shell Oil for $3.65 billion, immediately increasing the value of Mrs. Buck's trust to over $250 million. By the mid 1980s, the trust comprised approximately three-quarters of the total assets of the San Francisco Foundation.

Meanwhile, Marin County became one of the wealthiest counties in the nation, with a per-capita income some 50 percent higher than any other county supported by the foundation. In 1984, the trustees of the San Francisco Foundation applied to alter the terms of the gift, requesting permission to distribute some funds to other counties while maintaining priority for the needs of Marin County residents.[7] They cited the *cy pres* doctrine and Mrs. Buck's general charitable intent.

These efforts proved unsuccessful, as the California courts held that the trustees were unable to demonstrate that it was impossible or impracticable to follow Mrs. Buck's wishes, as required by *cy pres*. Today the funds are managed by the Marin County Community Foundation. Total assets exceed $1 billion and they are spent in Marin County. The foundation funds a local institute on aging and another devoted to the health of young people and issues of substance abuse, as well as programs in housing and many others. (It should be noted that California has yet to adopt the amended UTC code.)

Despite these emerging precedents, the doctrines of *cy pres* and deviation are alive and well in the courts. Our picture would not be complete without mention of two highly publicized cases that have tested the strength of donor intent: the Barnes Foundation case and the Leona Helmsley estate. In the former case, the courts ultimately sided with the trustees who determined to change the intent of the donor. The case revolved around the explicit wishes of Albert Barnes concerning the location and presentation of his valuable modern art collection in suburban Philadelphia. The trustees petitioned to relocate the collection to a new facility in downtown Philadelphia. In a decision culminating a decade of litigation, the Pennsylvania Orphan's Court concluded that there was "no viable alternative" to the move in light of the costs associated with maintaining and curating the collection.*

In the Helmsley case, the trustees of the charitable trust created with her $5 billion-plus estate also petitioned the courts seeking permission to extend the purposes of the trust beyond "the welfare of animals," as she had specified in a mission statement drafted before her death. Their petition was supported by the attorney general of the state of New York. The court ruled that this mission statement had not been officially incorporated into the documents establishing her trust and that the trustees had sole discretion to apply the trust to charitable purposes as they saw fit.[8]

The one constant in all these cases, no matter the outcome, is that litigation over donor intent is always costly and uncertain in its outcome. Determination and financial investment are required to pursue claims to enforce donor intent. While the general trend of verdicts is positive for donors,

---

* Chris Abbinante's 1997 article in the *University of Pennsylvania Law Review* discusses the entire history of the litigation in considerable detail and concludes that the courts and the trustees of the Barnes Foundation erred in their judgment. So does Martin Wooster. For the record, I was a lucky visitor to the extraordinary Barnes Collection in its suburban home on many occasions. Whatever one thinks of the ruling, don't miss the chance to see the collection in its new home!

the litigation is always protracted—and findings are often reversed upon appeal. In general, however, the courts do seem sympathetic to donors (or their survivors) when recipients take it upon themselves to make changes in the uses of gifts without careful consultation with other interested parties.

Legal thinkers have strong opinions on this issue. Some have even proposed a for-profit monitoring company to enforce trustee compliance with donor wishes. Judge Richard Posner has reasoned that the entire dichotomy is false:

> Since no one can foresee the future, a rational donor knows that his intentions might eventually be thwarted by unpredictable circumstances and may therefore be presumed to accept implicitly a rule permitting modification of the terms of the bequest in the event that an unforeseen change frustrates his original intention.[9]

Others have reached quite different conclusions. In "Interpreting the Founder's Vision," Judge Robert Bork draws a robust parallel between the role of federal judges and that of foundation trustees. Both groups, he argues, draw their power solely from the intent of those who created their roles, i.e., the nation's Founders or the philanthropist who created the foundation. They have a moral obligation to act only on this intent, rather than on their own ideas or values, especially because they are not directly accountable to anyone else in their privileged role.[10]

Bork takes exception to the very idea of trustees deviating from a donor's intent in the public interest, arguing that this notion disguises what trustees are really doing, that is, engaging in politics in the culture wars of the moment, as he puts it. Here they will inevitably act on their own—rather than the original donor's values—and in Bork's opinion, the "semi-skilled intellectuals" who make up foundation boards are generally egalitarian, redistributionist, and morally relativistic—values he clearly opposes.

Bork goes so far as to suggest that it should be illegal for a philanthropist to grant *carte blanche* to trustees to spend the money as the trustees see fit, as such noted philanthropists as Rockefeller, MacArthur, Ford, and, more recently, Warren Buffett have done. But Bork ends up admitting that "there are few effective ways of enforcing the stated intentions against foundation officers who ignore the donor's desires."

Bork's strong views lead me to ponder the issue from a different perspective. What are the personal responsibilities of the donor when it comes to creating a perpetual private foundation?

Donor Intent and Donor Responsibility

Donors have complete and absolute freedom to do with their fortunes as they wish. The only catch is that they cannot also enjoy favorable tax treatment of these same fortunes. If they seek such treatment through a foundation, they must surrender the right to reclaim their money; they must submit to certain minimum spending and reporting requirements; and so on. Whether one views these administrative/legal constraints as invasive or appropriate, there is a larger question to be addressed: how deserving of continuation, in perpetuity, are the charitable intentions of the donor?

Our first inclination, I suspect, is to assume that all donor intentions are worthy. Curtis W. Meadows, Jr., estate lawyer and president emeritus of the Meadows Foundation, offers this moving quotation from a student paper he received while teaching at the University of Texas:

> A charitable gift is an expression of individualism. To make a charitable gift is to make a statement about one's self and one's own values. . . . It is the quest for individualism which, in my opinion, is the strongest motivator driving Americans to give as they do. . . . [E]ven the smallest gift carries a symbolic value that tells, in one way or another, something about the character and the worldview of the giver.[11]

Not all philanthropists, however, spend time and effort recording their personal perspectives on these noble ideas. Waldemar Nielsen, one of the original trustees of the Ford Foundation, notes that the trustees hired a team of lawyers to search Henry Ford's papers for guidance about his philanthropic ideas after his death: "After the most comprehensive combing of the family and company papers, these people from the law firm were unable to find a single sentence or a single note from old Henry expressing any interest in, or ideas about, his philanthropy."[12] They found instead a number of thoughts about how charity weakened the will of men to work hard. In Ford's case, the foundation was, as least in part, about keeping control of the company in the hands of family members. Nielsen goes on to suggest that those who have criticized the decisions of Ford Foundation trustees as being out of line with Ford's personal values are instead expressing their personal values concerning philanthropy, rather than offering a justified criticism of the Ford trustees straying from donor intent. Donors, Nielsen points out, are no more consistent and rational than investors or any other group of humans.* *Homo philanthropicus* is as much a fiction as *homo economicus.* So any effort, no matter how well intentioned, to adhere to donor intent long after a donor's death is a purely speculative enterprise on the part of the trustees. How can anyone know what a given donor would do under different circumstances in a different era?† It appears that the Bork argument can cut both ways.

---

* Martin Wooster reviews the convoluted history of the Ford Foundation, the Ford family, the state of Michigan, and the Ford trustees in *The Great Philanthropists and the Problem of Donor Intent* (Washington, D.C.: Capital Research Center, 2008), 26–46. He takes a different line from Meadows, suggesting that the trustees have deviated from Ford's implied intentions, while admitting that Ford left no explicit instructions.

† I do not mean to suggest that trustees should not make every possible effort to carry out their responsibilities toward the donors' intentions. Certainly the vast majority of first- and second-generation trustees make every effort to do so, just as the original Ford trustees presumably did. A fine example of new trustee diligence is found at the Daniels Fund in Denver, established by cable television pioneer Bill Daniels. See http://www.danielsfund.org. I believe that the issue becomes infinitely more complex as the generations pass.

Nielsen and Meadows also comment on the lived reality of foundation creation. In their experience, philanthropic thinking is sometimes put off until the grim reaper is near and the donor is no longer able to articulate, for perpetuity, his or her charitable intentions. The task of choosing the most effective and dependable trustees is likewise beyond the donor's capability. Grand ideas arrived at on short notice with little research are not likely to represent the best thinking even of worthy individuals.

Meadows lists the many stakeholders involved in the philanthropic process and notes the inevitable conflicting interests that arise among donors, lawyers, trustees, foundation staff, and grant recipients, as well as the IRS and the appropriate state attorney general over the course of many decades. He underscores the variability of individual behavior noted by Nielsen and concludes that any attempt to use the life of the donor as a guide to philanthropic intent is generally an exercise filled with ambiguity and interpretation.

A donor who is genuinely philanthropic and concerned about his or her intentions must work to develop these intentions during his or her lifetime. The more thoughtfully this guidance is developed and articulated, the more useful it will be to future trustees. If not prepared to give one's money away during one's life—thereby ensuring that the task is done exactly as one wishes—one must invest time and thought in order to provide responsible guidance to future trustees.

While there is certainly nothing wrong with the charge offered by John D. Rockefeller to "promote the well-being of mankind throughout the world," such boilerplate wording simply shifts complete responsibility for philanthropic giving to future trustees. Examples of those philanthropists who successfully defined areas of focus for future trustees while allowing latitude for change include Robert Wood Johnson, Alfred Sloan, and, of course, Andrew Carnegie.[13] Donors frequently specify a geographic area or an institution for their intended philanthropy. Such guidance would seem completely unambiguous. But institutions and geographies do change over time, often radically (recall the Buck Trust story), so once again the decision requires careful thought and perhaps considerable research. All prudent benefactors will recognize that it is probably impossible to ensure exact adherence to very detailed wishes in perpetuity.*

Trustee selection also requires careful thought. Given that these individuals will have complete authority over the execution of the donor's wishes, the choice is a momentous one. In many cases, donors carry out this important responsibility with care and wisdom. Alfred Sloan did exactly that by including several of his fellow GM executives on the board of his foundation, ensuring a businesslike concern for impact and outcomes in his foundation's grant-making. On the other hand, Meadows cites many cases of family foundations established by donors in the hope of uniting members of their families around a charitable enterprise. Such ventures are sel-

---

* Some prominent philanthropists, such as Sir John Templeton, have certainly invested both time and money in attempting to do so. Only time will tell how effective these efforts may be.

dom successful, in his judgment, when there is little family cohesion to begin with. The foundation becomes the playing field on which family conflicts are played out.

All these issues are closely tied, of course, to the very idea of a gift in perpetuity. It is profoundly difficult for any person, no matter how smart or successful, to see the future clearly enough to know the best use of his or her fortune many generations in the future. It is also true that a gift in perpetuity means that a much smaller amount of money is immediately available to the chosen cause, perhaps limiting the impact on current, urgent needs. This recognition may account for the growing popularity of "giving while living" as a philanthropic philosophy. It may also explain the growing use of time-limited foundations, as noted in Lenz and Wolcheck's 2009 study.[14]

On the other hand, most significant problems in our society do not yield to large, one-time expenditures of money. Solutions require persistence and determination over time, and a perpetual foundation has just such a perspective. In an age when we have come to expect instant resolution of our problems, it is undoubtedly valuable to our social progress to have the experience and continuity of dedicated foundations over decades with the promise of perpetuity. We are clearly fortunate to have developed a system of private foundations to supplement the daily generosity of private citizens in building our social well-being. We are also fortunate that all these donors have some two million options to donate their money to today, and we can only hope that there is no movement to limit or restrict the number of such 501(c)(3) organizations going forward. As Meadows notes:

> The fundamental right of every American citizen to engage in his or her own individual philanthropic selection and action is the foundation of the giving spirit of our voluntary nonprofit system. As a free people we want the right to live our lives with as much freedom and individual choice as possible, including the making and selection of philanthropic and charitable choices. Yet freedom always comes with the possibility of abuse and the need for responsible voluntary actions and choices, if restrictions of the freedoms are to be avoided.[15]

In conclusion, then, adherence to donor intent enjoys broad support in America, as well it should given its centrality to our tradition of citizen-to-citizen generosity. It is hard to imagine that any effort, legislative or otherwise, could prevail against the great multiplicity of court actions that would rise up in every state to defend the freedom of foundations to mind donor intent as far as is practicable. The expense and extended litigation necessary to attack donor intent would never be worthwhile, even if the chances of success were more likely than American history shows them to be. As Joel Fleishman put it in the citation that opens this book, "The core strength of American foundations is not in the amount of money they give away, but in their Constitution-given right to disburse it with absolute autonomy, subject only to non-substantive, process-oriented legal restrictions." He believes that donor intent is protected as free speech under the First Amendment. I believe he is right.

CHAPTER EIGHT

Contemporary Criticisms of Private Foundations

It is tempting to argue that the world of private foundations should be exactly that—private. If individuals are generous enough to donate their fortunes to causes for the greater good, who would have the nerve to find fault? Yet such reasoning is simply wishful thinking in an increasingly transparent, opinionated, and networked age. In this chapter I provide a brief summary of contemporary criticisms of private foundations—without, for the moment, editorial comments. This survey will provide important insights into the ongoing relationships among foundations, governmental bodies, and advocacy groups. It is a natural complement to the history of foundation activities and of regulation provided in earlier chapters.

Of course I do have some personal thoughts on the merits of these various critiques. I will include them in Part III.

Generosity Unbound

Criticisms of What Private
Foundations Do (or Don't Do)

Criticism I:
Foundations should spend more
of their assets now

The remarkable asset run-ups of the past decade or two, even punctuated with periodic bursting of economic bubbles, have led to very large asset accumulations in foundations, with the Bill and Melinda Gates Foundation leading the way.* Critics feel that private foundations should spend more of their assets more rapidly given the dimensions of current needs.†

University endowments have also been targeted for criticism because of their exponential growth in recent decades. Under such pressure, the wealthiest institutions—such as Harvard, Princeton, and Yale, with endowments in the tens of billions of dollars—have modified their financial-aid programs, replacing loans to students in need with outright grants in aid. These decisions are made by university trustees. (Williams College trustees recently voted to rescind such a program in the wake of the 2008 financial downturn.)

---

* See the discussion of the 1969 tax law on page 156.

† See Pablo Eisenberg, "What's Wrong with Charitable Giving and How to Fix It," *Wall Street Journal*, November 9, 2009. The counter-argument—that foundations risk depleting their assets through this approach and may be unable to address future, perhaps unforeseen problems effectively as a result—is hardly trivial.

Chapter Eight

Criticism II: Foundations are not investing in the areas of greatest need

Starting with the assumption that all foundations are required to act for the common good because of their favored tax status, critics posit that foundations should deploy significant resources to address the immediate needs of the widest possible cross-section of citizens. This mission is in keeping with the Constitution's injunction to "promote the general welfare." Giving to the poor and marginalized amounts to only 10–15 percent of foundation total giving, according to these critics, even when indirect benefits from medical research and the like are included.[1] This number, they contend, does not meet the test of serving the greater good.

Every foundation, in this view, is obliged to pursue inclusivity, and every mission—no matter how narrowly framed by a donor—should be adapted to meet a common-good definition. Thus, a foundation devoted to animal welfare should support the involvement of underrepresented minorities in veterinary education. An arts foundation should ensure museum access for poor and marginalized kids. A medical-research foundation should support approaches to disease that cover the widest and most diverse patient populations.[2]

These critics assert that too much private philanthropy flows to activities and institutions deemed

189

self-serving for the well-to-do: museums, private liberal arts colleges and Ivy League universities, concert halls, and land trusts to protect wealthy suburbs.

Criticism III: Foundations are not making as big an impact with their investments as they should

This criticism can be heard from many voices across the political spectrum. A recent survey by the Philanthropy Awareness Initiative found that 85 percent of those surveyed (influential individuals who served on boards of not-for-profits in their communities) could not name a foundation that was benefitting their community.[3] This would seem an odd state of affairs for foundations seeking to make a difference.

This criticism focuses on foundation impact, or the lack thereof. Impact, in turn, is dependent on the criteria for success that are agreed upon when funding is provided for a given project. This view implies that an organized, businesslike mindset should be applied to the philanthropic enterprise. To operate efficiently and maximize the benefits of their investments, foundations should embrace a rigorous process of goal-setting, strategic planning, and measurement of results. All this begins with self-education on the part of those responsible for dispensing funds. Perhaps the most elaborate critique formulated from this perspective is that of

Paul Brest and Hal Harvey, as articulated in their book *Money Well Spent.*[4]

Brest and Harvey use the term "strategic philanthropy" to describe the approach they advocate. Foundation investments should drive meaningful change to improve society, rather than simply dispense money to worthy causes. To have impact, a foundation must develop a "theory of change," a view of what needs to happen for permanent improvements to occur in its chosen area(s) of investment. Grant-making must be guided by such a coherent theory. Results must be measured objectively, implying that foundations should invite external evaluation of their programs. When a program fails to meet expectations, all parties, including foundation officers, are expected to ask difficult and candid questions about the reasons for failure in the spirit of learning from mistakes. Organizations have arisen to facilitate this evaluative process.[5]

An additional criticism of contemporary foundations is closely related to the issue of successful grant-making. It has to do with the (poor) management of tension between risk and successful programs. Critics argue that too many foundations err on the side of low-risk projects. It is natural for foundations, intent on using their resources wisely, to fund projects that offer the greatest chances of success, according to the criteria established at the outset. Yet social change is by definition a high-risk undertaking. One does not seek to help habitual drug users, the incarcerated, or overweight children without recognizing that there will be many failures at the individual level. Achieving the proper balance between risk and prudence is an issue for every board of trustees.

Criticisms of How Private Foundations Operate

In addition to the conceptual criticisms noted above, a number of operational shortcomings have been noted by contemporary critics. Many of these objections are made by those who depend on foundations for funds to carry out their work.

Criticism I: Lack of transparency

The only way for foundations to protect the freedom, creativity, and flexibility they now enjoy is to open their doors and windows to the world so that all can see what they are doing and how they are doing it.

–Joel Fleishman[6]

Transparency is often a code word for trust. Complaints about self-dealing in the private foundation world rise when the public trust is shaken. Human beings are fallible, and there are always too many examples of abuses—most recently in well-publicized cases with the Red Cross and the United Way of

Washington, D.C., among others.[7] Moreover, the public generally holds those in the philanthropic world to a higher standard than those in private-sector commerce. General public anxiety—about national security, jobs, health care, and the like—only contributes to the weakening of trust in those who control large sums of money.

As public trust is diminished, there have been various calls over the years for an independent watchdog to supervise foundations.[8] Some have recommended government oversight in the form of a national charities board, as in the United Kingdom. The federal government does require all foundations, as well as 501(c)(3)s, to file an annual report that details their activities, including grants made and funds expended. A number of enterprising Web-based services now gather and array these filings for easy examination by the public.

These efforts are a harbinger of our highly networked future, according to Venture Philanthropy Partners founder Mario Morino.[9] In his view, transparency will become a fact of life for all entities, whether they embrace the notion or not. It is no longer necessary, Morino points out, to organize a formal agency for the watchdog function to occur. Thousands of bloggers and information aggregators are making it happen—for consumer products and government regulators alike—on a daily basis. There is no reason to think that private foundations will be exempt from this trend. Donees will have every chance to speak truth to power for all the world to hear. The Gates Keepers blog, for instance, is already up and running tracking the Gates Foundation.

Criticism II: Foundations operate in isolation

Foundations have been criticized for being out of touch with those they wish to help from the time that the first foundations were established. In late-nineteenth-century America, the lives of the working poor seldom intersected with those of the well-to-do. It fell to such creative thinkers as Jane Addams and Lillian Wald (among the nation's first female college graduates) to bridge the gap by taking up residence among immigrants in settlement houses. Grace Dodge, a wealthy philanthropist and accomplished listener, did likewise through her working-girls clubs that became a national phenomenon. A short time later, Julius Rosenwald traveled throughout the rural South to discuss community needs directly with the sharecropper citizens he wished to help.

Contemporary critics offer a variant on the out-of-touch theme. Those who advocate increased diversity among the staff and leadership of private foundations imply that the presence of more people from marginalized groups will help to bridge the cultural and racial gaps that they feel exist today.

Another dimension of being out-of-touch, critics argue, is a certain disregard on the part of foundations for the operating realities of the organizations that apply to foundations for support. Let's consider this latter criticism first.

Criticism III:
Lack of donor-centered operating procedures

The transparency issues noted above can refer to issues such as executive compensation, board compensation, the affiliations of trustees, and the like. It can also encompass the decision-making process for grants, as in the case when unsuccessful fund seekers are provided with no guidance or feedback on reasons for their failure. Critics ask that foundations align and make transparent their program priorities so that potential grant-seekers are in possession of the clearest and most useful information during the application process. Changing a foundation's priorities requires careful timing and intensive communication efforts with would-be grant-seekers.

Other operating procedures singled out for criticism by those seeking support from private foundations: 1) complex application processes that are overly time-consuming for under-resourced organizations; 2) failure or unwillingness to provide grants to cover general-operating purposes; 3) failure or unwillingness to fund extended time periods; 4) slow payments and slow response times; and 5) decision-making by trustees on an annual or semi-annual basis that leaves dependent organizations in a perpetual state of waiting (rolling decisions could cure this issue).

Criticism IV: Lack of leadership diversity

The Greenlining Institute argues that diversity in foundation leadership leads to diversity in grant-making. They cite data showing that almost 50 percent of grants made to minority-led organizations in 2005 in California came from the ten foundations with the most diverse boards of directors. This perspective argues for "diversity of race, ethnicity, income, gender, and even sexual orientation" among foundation leadership teams *and* among grant recipients.

All such categorization efforts have their critics as well. These categories are easily deconstructed, as the academics say. What exactly does minority-led mean for an organization? The poor can be categorized by income level, by a lack of opportunity (those with low odds of achieving certain basic educational milestones, health outcomes, or employment goals), or even potentially dismissed entirely by reference to a scorecard of material possessions.

Diversity is another term that is fraught with complexity. Advocacy groups argue for or against support to many additional categories of diversity, such as age, geography,* and religious beliefs, in addition to those already enumerated in the definition of marginalized. It is certainly plausible to add donor diversity to the list of diversities. Religious diversity, for instance, has characterized the donor community in America for almost two hundred years. Catholic philanthropy developed in the 1820s and 1830s in conjunction with the waves of working-class immigrants from Europe and the Caribbean and the establishment of the first religious orders in the United States.[10] Jewish philanthropy, with its exemplary traditions based in the teachings of Maimonides about Tsedakah, has flourished in America in the twentieth century.

The diversity of our nation's ethnic and racial mix continues to develop with the addition of diverse Hispanic, Asian, Middle Eastern, and African groups. These newer arrivals add larger numbers of Muslims and the teachings on generosity from the Koran. It is surely a matter of considerable importance that our American traditions of citizen generosity engage the practices of generosity of these new Americans and that a richer amalgam be cultivated among all of us.

---

* We remember the term "Eastern Establishment" from the 1950s and 1960s. As noted in chapter three, private foundations today have a much broader geographic distribution. Critics argue that rural areas remain underserved by foundations.

Conclusion

These criticisms, both conceptual and operational, testify to the health and vitality of our philanthropic enterprise. Large numbers of people are engaged in the effort to improve our nation and complete the work of the Founders. We may never achieve the ideals that they set forth, but we have ever larger numbers of people, more private financial resources, more experience, and better tools to address the challenge. But we also require trust among the interested parties if we are to move forward, and I sense that our shared trust is as fragile today as it was back in the 1960s. So in the next chapter, I want to share an idea about rebuilding this much-needed trust and executing the next steps in our pursuit of a more perfect Union.

Part III

Generosity Unbound: A Proposal
for a Declaration Initiative

Economics cannot finally resolve the most profound questions at the center of peoples' struggles as individuals, as families, and as a nation. Who are we? What must we do? How shall we live? What is right? When all the statistical analyses have been rendered, people still have to sit back and ask such questions . . . knowing what is right will be the least of . . . [our] problems. Doing what is right will be the key difficulty, and that is not mainly an intellectual issue.

–Glenn C. Loury,
"The Economics of Racial Equality and Justice"

CHAPTER NINE

A Framework

The economist Glenn Loury identifies the challenge we face: "What do we do with what we know?" Having traced the history of American generosity, how do we animate the lessons embedded in the Founders' synthesis of wealth-building and civic virtue in the twenty-first century? What special role can private foundations play at this particular time in American history?

The most important lesson from the Founders is that American citizens can shape the future when we unite around a shared moral ambition. In the Declaration of Independence, the signers drafted the mission statement for the new Union. We are their trustees. It is our responsibility to carry out their intent for the Union as one part of our personal responsibilities. After all, the Founders made the Union an important part of the mission of their lives. As we have seen, we have a great tradition of citizens working to honor the intent expressed in the Declaration. There is much more to be done, and we have an ideal moment to reunite around those high ideals of the Declaration.

On July 4, 2026, we will all celebrate the 250th anniversary of the signing of the Declaration of Independence. This approaching milestone offers an opportunity to recommit to those ideals on which our democracy is based. We need to engage as many citizens as possible in the ongoing challenge of making these ideals a reality for the largest number of American citizens.

I believe that our philanthropic sector, especially the leadership of private foundations, is best positioned to lead our national thinking on a Declaration Initiative. Foundation leaders understand that America is a value proposition based on the link between generosity and prosperity, both driven by America's entrepreneurial spirit. They understand the responsibilities of trusteeship. They are our custodians of mutuality and generosity. They are our civic leaders and often our business leaders as well. Foundation leaders have extensive experience as private citizens in building the nation's civic fabric. They are also aware of the multitude of private initiatives underway that are advancing equality of opportunity for all citizens and could perhaps become part of a larger national effort. Finally, based on my research for *Generosity Unbound*, I am convinced that these leaders share a broad set of beliefs that provide a basis for planning and collaboration.

For instance, most foundation leaders believe in the power of citizens to create effective solutions to social problems. They respect the marketplace of ideas in which thousands upon thousands of "little platoons" of citizens compete for resources to fund their better ideas. They believe that this marketplace should be strengthened and that the best ideas for improving the lives of citizens seldom come directly from the government.

These leaders share a deep appreciation of our democratic process. They would be able to model constructive citizen leadership. They understand that even in the world of tweets and sound bites, democracy requires a sustained discussion engaging multiple points of view to produce the wisest outcomes. I have faith that foundation leaders also recognize that the American dream of middle-class security is fragile and under constant threat. The current systems in place to support this voyage, whether health care, education, home ownership, or even the penal system, are in need of fresh thinking.

These discussions might begin by examining a potential set of shared beliefs, such as the following:

- the nation must continue pursuit of the Declaration's ideal, that all men are created equal and endowed by their Creator with rights to life, liberty, and the pursuit of happiness;
- while this ideal is available to the majority of Americans today, our poorest citizens still lack access to this promise;

- the poorest Americans face physically and socially fatal disparities that foreclose their chances of experiencing their inalienable rights;
- thousands of foundations, both alone and as partners, have been working with considerable success at mitigating these disparities;
- a larger middle class including independent, stable families would stabilize American communities and reduce our national indebtedness;
- our civic spirit and patriotism would be strengthened by a public declaration of Americans' unified efforts to fulfill an important part of our Founders' intent;
- as many citizens as possible should participate in advancing the Declaration's ideals.

Assuming such shared beliefs, it seems natural that our foundation sector could lead a national conversation on the importance of citizen leadership for equal access to inalienable rights. I am not calling for a large project or a monolithic shared programming effort. Quite the contrary, the great range and diversity of free philanthropic investments needs to remain the signal feature of American generosity. The upcoming anniversary offers an occasion to identify the efforts underway to advance the Founders' ideals. This Initiative would have an entrepreneurial structure, operate at the local level, and enable people to find dignity and independence as they strive toward middle-class well-being.

Such a project might capture the imagination of the nation just as the March of Dimes did in the first half of the twentieth century. No one could have predicted the transformative impact of that national ambition to end polio. In the teeth of the Great Depression, the March raised four billion dimes. We still feel its power in our lives from the generations of microbiologists who emerged from the graduate fellowships it funded. Those scientists and their protégés eventually produced the vaccinations that eliminated the killer diseases from young children's lives, advanced cancer research, and accelerated the discoveries that made HIV/AIDS a chronic rather than a fatal disease for those who can access the new generations of medications. Who could have imagined?

The March of Dimes offered a concrete goal that captured the imagination of millions of Americans. A Declaration Initiative would need the same bold vision and measurable goals, but its own twenty-first-century structure. It would require more moral ambition than new money. It would demand significant willingness to work productively across the full political spectrum and openness to including ways for many foundations and citizens—from grassroots rural and urban communities to corporate suites—to contribute the idealism that would make the 2026 celebration a meaningful event in American history.

A successful middle-class society depends on the capacity of its citizens to construct stable families, to provide for themselves and for their families, to access the benefits of society's institutions and resources, and to share voluntarily their resources with others. The engines of mutuality and middle-class self-sufficiency are inextricably linked in our democracy. Liberty, independence, and a philanthropic spirit thrive together. Philanthropic projects have been developed to address various aspects of the challenge of enabling all Americans to gain access to the education, housing, nutrition, job readiness, and even financial literacy that could enhance their progress to a better life. None of this is new. Declaration signers, most notably Benjamin Franklin and John Adams, recognized that these goals would demand values like industry and frugality as the basis of the household and of the economy.

The large number of foundation partnerships currently working to address the systems supporting advancement to the middle class makes the Declaration Initiative feasible. Examples of productive collaborations abound in the philanthropic sector. Bradley, MacArthur, Annie E. Casey, Edna McConnell Clark, Robert Wood Johnson, C. S. Mott, Kellogg, Hitachi, and the National Fund for Workforce Solutions, as well as a number of others, already devote substantial staff, board, and financial resources to issues related to upward mobility. They share philanthropic networks on specialized subjects from health care and pre-K–12 education to housing and asset-building. The Philanthropy Roundtable currently dedicates about one third of its resources to programs and publications on philanthropic strategies for opening up opportunity for low-income Americans. The Roundtable has offered its members numerous substantial programs on K–12 education. The leadership emphasizes approaches to achieving dramatic breakthroughs in the education of low-income children. Its members work easily across political boundaries.

The CityBridge Foundation heads, David and Katherine Bradley, have aligned their interests in advancing pre-K school readiness with the nationally acclaimed foundation efforts going on in their own city—such as KIPP, Teach for America, and D.C. PREP. Together with the Washington, D.C., superintendent, the foundations are attempting to assure a seamless high-quality education for low-income children. Together they are developing ways for all agendas to advance together, making everyone's investment count more. Money is not the whole story.

The full political spectrum is already engaged in this critical issue. Imagine if foundation executives expressly invited the rest of the philanthropic world, and all citizens, to join them in working toward the goals of the Declaration Initiative in their local communities, urban and rural, across the country. On July 4, 2026, the national celebration could prove profoundly meaningful. What if lives and prospects for liberty and the pursuit of happiness for the poorest Americans of 2010 were measurably better by 2026? What if these efforts were also saving the government hundreds of billions of dollars annually by that time?

The Challenging Current Environment

The nation faces challenging conditions today, as always. The recent Great Recession has seriously destabilized the economy. The significant levels of unemployment, mortgage foreclosures, and investment losses have harmed the security and mobility of citizens in all but the very highest income brackets. Moreover, giving may decline in 2010 as it did in 2008 and 2009, just when needs are more severe. These difficulties, I believe, make the case for launching an inspiring initiative to honor our Founders in 2026.

In addition, the country is experiencing high levels of partisanship and ideological polarization. This spirit has even spurred some modest but unseemly acts of violence against government leaders. Terrorism and two wars add to the nation's destabilized and fractious atmosphere. This environment has little that smacks of the optimism and patriotic pride that make both capitalism and philanthropy thrive.

Furthermore, we face a loss of urban civic leadership on the corporate side, through a combination of mergers, globalization, and suburbanization. This phenomenon of lost urban civic leaders—those who were called "the bishops" in their day in Hartford, Connecticut—has generated a search for solutions by urban community foundations. The urban studies scholar Carolyn Adams suggests replacing the civic leadership of local corporate executives with what she calls "meds and eds."[1] She reviews how executives from medical schools and higher education might play more powerful civic leadership roles in cities, given that their institutions are frequently among the largest employers, investors in land, and purchasers of goods and services in their regions. Great civic leadership is always a challenge. Philanthropic leaders are well placed to share the leadership challenge with business people, "meds and eds," and local clergy. If foundation leaders were to launch a Declaration Initiative, they might even redefine the concept of civic leadership.

We must confront another challenge to any declaration effort. It shows up in the field itself. Several of the leaders in philanthropy who advised me expressed discouragement about the state of the philanthropic sector. One well-respected colleague reported his serious "skepticism about modern philanthropy. To me it has lost its independence and imagination, its sense of creativity, and has become a junior partner of government, which undermines all those special features which you highlight in your manuscript." Unfortunately, this colleague is not the only one who expressed such pessimism. I heard this lament expressed with different caveats from leaders of politically conservative, liberal, and centrist foundations.

Such critiques deserve attention. First, unlike some of my advisors, I do find evidence of impressive creativity and imagination in philanthropy, maybe less than would be ideal, but we never have enough of these qualities anywhere. The eight-hundred-pound gorilla at the table is, of course, the government. The sheer size of the government's expenditures compared to the investments by philanthropy in social well-being is daunting. To be more specific, a study funded by the Department of Health and Human Services finds that the federal government spent 97 percent of its $720 billion allocation domestically for the six areas that overlap with philanthropic foundations' domestic spending.[2] (The missing 3 percent was spent internationally.) Therefore, while private foundations spent approximately $21 billion in 2006 within our borders for health, education, development, the environment, human services, and relief, the federal government spent roughly $700 billion—or just under thirty-three times the dollars the foundations spent.

Those who prefer that the government spend less, those who are satisfied with expenditures, and those who seek even larger tax-generated expenditures all agree that citizen generosity should remain a defining feature of American culture. For anyone who conceives of philanthropy as a dynamic marketplace of ideas where economic, intellectual, and cultural activity can flourish, the market dominance of one player is certainly daunting.

These findings are more or less troubling depending on one's personal philosophy and politics. Certainly the needs in a nation of over 310 million people are enormous and costly for the private philanthropic sector to bear alone. However, the nation's foundations do bring a unique asset to advancing the country's well-being. Historically, they have been more innovative, more responsive, faster moving, and more risk tolerant than the government. Interestingly, the launch of the Declaration Initiative could prove the ability of philanthropy to capture the national attention and imagination for a goal that conservatives, liberals, and centrists would be proud to help the country achieve. Creative solutions to enhance the systems of upward mobility also hold the promise of reducing, at least in part, the government cost burden in these areas.

Chapter Nine

Regardless of the challenging environment, America has a strong set of foundation leaders, who, I believe, share a set of basic principles. They also have access to a broad set of well-developed programs and research studies to use in designing the Declaration Initiative, as well as other assets to deploy. For instance, volunteer support could come from seniors and other able citizens. Most current citizens over sixty are children of the Greatest Generation and saw real patriotism at home. The generation currently under age forty did more volunteering in high school and college than any other generation in American history. Many Americans already understand the difference that volunteers make in our social-profit sector, and they might find it compelling to step up. In foundations and not-for-profit organizations, experienced senior staff members are surrounded by highly committed younger staff who are eager to change what is not optimal about modern philanthropy. We have a workforce ready to teach and to inspire.

Philanthropic leaders will want to develop their own plans to take back the "lost independence, imagination, and creativity" that some of their colleagues lament. The Initiative could be used to repair these fissures. To achieve the Declaration goals while also continuing the important work they are already pursuing, foundation leaders could seek to enlist a large percentage of the nation's 75,000 foundations in the effort. Every foundation has the potential to contribute. Our wealthiest organizations could begin some common efforts using a tiny percentage of their current funding and a large dose of entrepreneurial spirit.

The private foundation sector has championed the innovations that have become the new base cases in so many fields. Are we resourceful enough to invent (and adopt) a small dose of innovation in our own field? Many trustees I have consulted say that their foundations fund carefully planned work in specific areas. They also admit that they only rarely exchange information on the outcomes of the programs they fund, not even with other foundations working in the same or related fields.

We have the imagination to find a constructive way forward from current conflicts and environmental challenges. Foundations know a great deal more about effective problem solving than they did even twenty or thirty years ago. Many recognize the importance of a coherent "theory of change" to guide their investments.[3] Many also wish to be measured on their impact—i.e., on the outcomes of their investments in social change—rather than simply on their spending. Impact requires a commitment to setting measurable goals for improvement before, rather than after, a program is funded. It requires a willingness to participate in a process of listening to the field, offering feedback, collaborating on correction of processes where it is advisable, and pursuing continuous improvement.

That is what the Founders did for the colonies in their time. They imagined a whole different way for people to live. They took big risks, defined their mission, and negotiated hard across impossible differences. They left us the Union, the mission statement, and a world of aspirations we have pledged ourselves to pursue. When Glenn Loury writes:

"Who are we? What must we do? How shall we live? What is right? . . . [K]nowing what is right will be the least of . . . [our] problems. Doing what is right will be the key difficulty," he reminds me of a philosophy class I took in high school. The good sister who taught us stressed that God had given human beings three great gifts so we could do good in the world. We possessed the gifts of reason, imagination, and will. Reason equipped us to figure out what good was possible, imagination outfitted us to think beyond the immediately reasonable goods we could accomplish, and our wills had the power to direct us to actually do what reason and imagination had put in front of us.

So, what is reasonable for us to imagine we can do as members of the philanthropic sector? Our country needs us to help the economy recover and expand the middle class. Aristotle wrote that democracy needs a large majority of citizens to be comfortable or else its institutions will begin to break down. A profound gap between poorest and wealthiest is not healthy for our democracy. Private foundations can invent and invest in new ways to expand the gains of the middle class. Venture philanthropists have already initiated some of this work. My convent training convinced me of the power of reason, imagination, and will to renew the face of the Earth. Sister was always right.

Imagine that it is July 4, 2026. The nation is decorated with red, white, and blue bunting and the fireworks begin to go off. Imagine that the middle class in America has been greatly increased. Childhood poverty is a historical artifact in

2026, the way child labor was back in 1926. Many, many citizens feel special pride in having participated in a process that created real social progress and also helped relieve enormous pressures on the federal budget.

What if private foundations had cultivated such a national ambition and then led the fifteen-year effort? Is it possible to imagine a more fitting tribute to the idealism and wisdom of the Founders? Would there be a stronger sign of our national gratitude for our Union? From all the evidence I have examined, I believe that private foundations have the wisdom, imagination, and will to make this happen.

This land which we have watered with our tears and our blood is now our mother country.

–Bishop Richard Allen, Founder,
African Methodist Episcopal Church

CHAPTER TEN

Defining the Need

Why should leaders from the private-foundation sector take on voluntarily the design and implementation of a Declaration Initiative? The answer is clear: because it is sorely needed by our fellow citizens, by our economy, and by our reputation for moral leadership in the world.

Our democracy is based on the idea of liberty and justice for all. There are still today entirely too many citizens blocked from accessing the promises of the Declaration of Independence. Moral leadership could intervene to change this situation.* A significant increase in the number of citizens

---

* More than four decades after the United States government declared "war on poverty," the official 2008 poverty rate was 12.3 percent, not even 2 percent less than the 1967 figure of 14.2. Report from the National League of Cities, "Poverty and Economic Insecurity: Views from City Hall," http://www.nlc.org/ASSETS/D6A52A2214A84F1EA208A18CDA25D83D/ExecutiveSummary.pdf.

reaching the income and security levels of the middle class would greatly reduce the fatal disparities that afflict so many of our nation's children from birth.*

Fatal disparities abort opportunities for life, liberty, and the pursuit of happiness. They outright kill people and kill their chances for a good life. High infant-mortality rates have been documented among lower-income populations for more than 130 years.[1] While rates have improved overall, unacceptable differences persist.[2] The education of mothers matters a great deal to the survival of babies to their first birthdays.

Similarly, children from families with the fewest resources are already headed toward social death when they arrive at kindergarten with one-third the usable vocabulary of children from middle- and upper-income ones.[3] They rarely catch up. Statistically, girls walk their path to early pregnancies, abortions, maybe drugs or alcohol, dropping out of school, and often abusive relationships with the men in their lives. Boys walk the male version of the same path, but more often end up in prison—and out, and in again.

Disparities persist for high school completion, incarceration, and longevity. Our democracy puts these persistent inequalities in citizens' hands to redress, if we take seriously the Founders' commitments. Continuing inequalities in our nation do not reflect well on the land of the free and the home

---

* I am well aware that poverty does not spare older Americans, for instance, nor is poverty concentrated in urban areas, as we often imagine. Much is hidden by rural geography and it is essential that we diversify our efforts across geographies and age categories. Poverty has as many faces as there are people and places in America.

of the brave. These disparities constitute high-value targets for remediation. We can establish measurable goals for reducing such disparities with relative ease. Reaching these goals, in turn, would translate into very high levels of economic, as well as social, benefit to the nation.

No one seems to know how we can sustain our budgets' multiple entitlement commitments for much longer. Moreover, there seems to be little political will on either side of the aisle to make difficult decisions. Philanthropists and concerned citizens have an opportunity to help our nation's economy because, when people live significantly better, they do not require government expenditures. Many costs in our means-tested social support programs could be reduced or eliminated as our middle class grows. The economic cost of addressing the problems poverty creates is enormous, and these costs are, of course, borne by all of us. Of greater moral importance are the costs in human suffering, wasted potential, and the fraying of our social fabric.

"Just" the elimination of childhood poverty and its consequences in America could reduce current costs to the U.S. budget by up to half a trillion dollars. Imagine if the work of the philanthropic sector could contribute this gift to the nation. The Initiative has this potential. Poverty has a disproportionate impact on children. Children represent 25 percent of the total population in the U.S., but 35 percent of the poorest population.[4] A total of 14.1 million children—or 19 percent of all U.S. children—are poor, and the distribution is highly skewed by race, as well as by geography: 10.6 percent of white, non-Hispanic children are poor, while 33.9 percent of black children and 30.6 of Hispanic children fall into this category.[5]

A recent study, "The Economic Costs of Poverty in the United States: Subsequent Effects of Children Growing Up Poor,"[6] reviews research on the relationship between children growing up poor and their earnings, propensity to commit crime, and quality of health later in life. It includes estimates of costs per person that crime and poor health impose on the economy. The average costs per child are then aggregated across the total number of children growing up in poverty in the U.S. This process enables researchers to estimate the total costs of child poverty to the U.S. economy.

The conclusions reached by this study can be summarized as follows:

> The costs to the U.S. associated with childhood poverty total about $500 billion per year, or the equivalent of nearly 4 percent of GDP. More specifically, we estimate that childhood poverty each year:
> - reduces productivity and economic output by about 1.3 percent of GDP;
> - raises the costs of crime by 1.3 percent of GDP;
> - raises health expenditures and reduces the value of health by 1.2 percent of GDP.[7]

"In other words," the authors conclude, "we could raise our overall consumption of goods and services and our quality of life by about a half trillion dollars a year if childhood poverty were eliminated. If anything, this calculation likely understates the true annual losses associated with U.S. poverty."[8] Such enormous potential for annual tax savings would be reason enough to launch a Declaration Initiative, even if the moral call to social justice and the Founders' aspirations for our democracy were not so compelling in themselves.

Second, private foundation leaders should consider this work because our democracy is based on a Constitution that makes us responsible as "We the people . . . to establish Justice, insure domestic Tranquility, provide for the common defence, provide for the general Welfare, and secure the Blessings of Liberty to ourselves and our posterity. . . ." That sounds like a call to action. And it seems that our democracy is very much in need of greater unified action.

A successful Declaration Initiative would also demonstrate to the nation and the world that Tocqueville's "civic associations" still have power and meaning in the twenty-first century. They do have enormous force in America today, as we are all well aware. But too many citizens simply do not grasp their importance or see them simply as lobbying organizations trying to get federal dollars for their constituencies—like everyone else. The Initiative would enable "little platoons" to increase their visibility and their work together. Whether or not associations aligned specifically with the goals of the Initiative, they would all benefit from increased recognition as important contributors to the quality of civic life in America. The field of philanthropy would be better understood and better appreciated if its national leaders led a public effort to create real equality for all citizens. The idea of eliminating fatal disparities harbors the very American idealism that could boost the nation's dampened spirit. Can we imagine private citizens in any other nation undertaking such an effort?

This thought brings me to the last reason why an initiative is a strong idea for America. The global reputation of our nation has begun to erode. Foundation leadership of a Declaration Initiative would surely capture the imagination of the international community and could shore up our shaky global image. Articles and books appear weekly analyzing how recent events spell the end of American world leadership. Few realize that America's hegemony is vested in her ideals, the concepts that the Founders embedded in our Declaration of Independence. Fewer still understand how seriously our citizens take those words.

"Globalization is striking back," writes Gabor Steingart, an editor at Germany's leading news magazine, *Der Spiegel*. As others prosper, he argues, the United States has lost key industries, its people have stopped saving money, and its government has become increasingly indebted to Asian central banks.[9] The financial crisis has only given greater force to such fears.

Fareed Zakaria, the contemporary scholar and journalist, published *The Post–American World* in 2008, in which he calls the "rise of the rest" a clear challenge to the power of the U.S. "Many look at the vitality of this emerging world and conclude that the United States has had its day. The particular rise of China as a global power buttresses the predictions of the prophets of doom." Zakaria remains guardedly optimistic because he finally concludes that the "rise of the rest" is part of what America has tried to engender since the Marshall Plan. Zakaria continues: "Over the last twenty years, globalization has been gaining depth and breadth. America has benefited massively from these trends. It has enjoyed unusually robust growth, low unemployment and inflation, and received hundreds of billions of dollars in investment." Nonetheless, he proposes that we face a curious problem. Other nations have begun to view the "rise of the rest" as the consequence of decline of the U.S. rather than as a sign of the economic and social improvements in the rising nations. The message from this part of Zakaria's work is that perceptions count a great deal.[10]

Another knowledgeable contemporary, James Fallows, has addressed this issue in "Can America Rise Again?" Fallows, who spent years living in China and reflecting on U.S. and global politics from that vantage point, insists on the importance of regaining global respect for our fiscal stability. "Would the world respect a threadbare America? Will repressive values rise with an ascendant China—and liberal values sink with a foundering United States? How much will American leaders have to kowtow?"[11]

Fallows recalls the warning of John Adams, who worried about the sustainability of virtue in men because wealth-building often bred greed. Adams wrote: "Remember, democracy never lasts long. It soon wastes, exhausts, and murders itself. There never was a democracy yet that did not commit suicide." We have to ask ourselves, are we there?

If we don't want our children and grandchildren to live in another kind of nation-state than our democracy, is there something we should do? Can we do it? We know that the last census in 2000 predicts that by 2030 the majority of the U.S. population under thirty-five will be "of color." More people of color still experience poverty than whites do. If an initiative could fix even parts of the systems designed to bring more people into our middle class, it would strengthen our country, our economy, our international reputation, and, of course, our chances of affirming the reality of our democracy's mission statement. I am reminded of the instruction I receive each time I board an airplane: " In case of a loss of cabin pressure, put on your own mask first before assisting others!"

I am not an alarmist, but I am not comforted by Niall Ferguson's recent article in *Foreign Affairs*, "Complexity and Collapse, Empires on the Edge of Chaos."[12] Ferguson focuses on the history of the fall of empires. While it may take centuries for an empire to rise from chaotic origins (think Rome, the Ming Dynasty, the Soviet Union, or Great Britain), Ferguson hypothesizes that empires can collapse precipitously, often in less than a decade. A destabilizing event occurs and the slowly deteriorating strengths of the empire cannot cope creatively or energetically with the event. A downward spiral ensues.

What is at stake for us now? I believe that America must survive as a global power in order for the ideals of human rights, justice for all, and entrepreneurial free markets to survive. China's population is four times that of the U.S. (1.3 billion versus 309 million). It is only logical that, barring some disaster, at some point in the future China's economy will be larger than ours. We are all better off if China progresses successfully. But the real test of America's global power is not the size of our economy, or even the might of our military. Both are important and cannot be weak. The real test is whether our people sustain our American values proposition—and whether people in other countries continue to want their children to become citizens of the U.S. This is the test of our moral leadership. It is the determinative characteristic of our country. The justice and fairness and opportunities that hard-working people can find here define the dreams of parents the world over. Our global hegemony rests on our moral leadership.

Ferguson asserts that, when empires fail rapidly, the smartest and wealthiest people are paying so much attention to their own best interests that they are blindsided by the social changes underway. No other empire, however, has been based on a sociopolitical system guided by "self-interest, rightly understood." American leaders, particularly those in the philanthropic sector, can leverage this advantage. Generosity at all levels can activate patriotism, address the needs of the poor, and strengthen our budget and our global standing. The engagement of American private foundation leaders in assuring the upward mobility of our poorest citizens would communicate forcefully that the Declaration's values remain in place. They would demonstrate that "self-interest, rightly understood" is alive and working. These enduring values, backed by generous collaborative action, are what sustain America's hegemony. The challenge is great and urgent.

I understand that in proposing an idea as grand as the Declaration Initiative, I am offering an optimistic version of the possible. I also understand that the many differences of mission and resources among foundations will create difficulties in implementing a shared project. Many will assume that the biggest impediment to a successful initiative will come from the political differences among conservative, centrist, and liberal foundation leadership. That may be. Many obstacles of all sorts certainly will arise. But none of these obstacles compare to those faced by the Founders.

We are very fortunate. We need to match the Founders idealistic efforts and to express our continuing gratitude. Such actions would define the essence of American exceptionalism.

Doing well is the result of doing good.
That's what capitalism is all about.

–Ralph Waldo Emerson

CHAPTER ELEVEN

Getting Started

Our private-foundation sector has provided exemplary leadership in fulfilling our Founders' intent over many generations. It has embodied the virtues, discipline, and entrepreneurial energy they envisioned in the citizenry. No other group of Americans is so well placed to take on a Declaration Initiative. Given congressional gridlock and Wall Street's loss of credibility, the leaders of the private-foundation sector may be the only remaining individuals who have the tested leadership skills, wisdom, experience, and financial strength to sustain the development of a more perfect union.

Perhaps some readers will be inspired to begin the dialogue necessary to develop the Declaration Initiative described earlier. Such dialogue could occur within the context of professional organizations such as the Council on Foundations or the Philanthropy Roundtable. It could also occur through informal meetings of interested foundation leaders. However these initial conversations begin, they would naturally involve an exploration of our shared principles and commitments. I have great confidence that foundation leaders have the experience necessary to develop the vision, goals, and operating pathways that would enable the Initiative to capture the imagination of many fellow citizens.

Here, for instance, are a small number of high-level observations about how an initiative might move forward. These ideas are based on the lessons of our philanthropic history.

1. Keep the focus on the marketplace of ideas:
   a. Identify the specific social problems that merit earliest attention and invite a free-market competition of ideas to address these concerns. Local solutions with strong evidence of early success should be considered for investment of growth capital.

2. Operate inclusively:
   a. Ensure that the demand side of the marketplace is robust and well understood.
   b. Favor those communities that are willing to co-invest—through volunteers and local funding—in looking for partnerships.

3. Organize a lean, decentralized project management structure:
   a. Mechanisms envisioned should offer maximum freedom for participant funders to develop and implement the work they request to undertake.
   b. A highly experienced group of advisors, evaluators, and organizers should be engaged and made available to participating communities by request.

4. Assure a strong communications plan:
   a. Call on the experience of foundations and professional organizations that have successfully engaged the nation's attention on important topics.

5. In due time:
   a. Establish a set of measurable goals for each problem within appropriate time frames.
   b. Develop an effective system to monitor progress and support faltering sites.

Keeping the Focus on the Marketplace

Once common principles and shared values that emerge from the nation's needs and from the Founders' words are developed, the marketplace of ideas should provide many different approaches to getting to the goal. The design/build phase of the Initiative would welcome fierce debates on the most appropriate tactics. In a spirit of social entrepreneurism, since all players bring their own funds to the table, multiple projects could be funded. May the most effective approaches win!

A good number of foundations currently have shovel-ready projects that address the challenges of fixing systems designed to move citizens toward the middle class. Robert Wood Johnson and Ford have for a number of years been training health paraprofessionals from low-income communities. These community health-care workers serve their own people in a variety of highly productive and personalized extensions of standard medical care. Evidence-based research has shown that some of these paraprofessionals can significantly increase levels of compliance by diabetics. The evaluations have shown that these interventions reduce blindness and amputations by 50 percent. Other community health workers are trained to support young mothers-to-be and advise on postpartum breast-feeding and infant care. Typically these members of the community visit their clients several times a month and deepen a relationship that creates positive reinforcements for better health and more promising futures at lower costs to the health-care system. Such programs also provide jobs with dignity for people who have often been consigned to lives of manual labor. Their education for these jobs raises the sights of community members and adds income flow to their areas.

School readiness projects, high school completion, and college prep projects also would merit attention. Some, such as the Nativity grammar schools and Christo Rey high schools sponsored by the Jesuit order, have been underway for thirty years and have built a record of achievement serving students from low-income communities all over the country. The foundation sector has also birthed full opportunity projects like the well-known Harlem Children's Zone led by Geoffrey Canada. And there are countless, lesser known programs across the country that deserve the opportunity to grow. A broader open marketplace, perhaps supported through enhanced technology, would serve to identify and mobilize such ideas.*

Including a Wide Range of Participants

Foundations know that meaningful change requires commitment from the bottom up as well as from the top down. Listening is a critical skill for all involved in the change process. Past foundation successes suggest wise approaches to achieving the productive involvement of all stakeholders. Moreover, this involvement must be more than symbolic and include both leadership and grassroots constituent presence.

Community foundations now number over seven hundred across the nation and have grown significantly in assets over the past twenty years. Their expertise in local funding and their deep knowledge of local operational issues create seven hundred natural allies in any initiative to eliminate fatal disparities. Community-foundation executives, donors, and boards would be powerful and well-informed collaborators in Initiative leadership.

---

* Both the Harlem Children's Zone and the Nurse Family Partnership have been recognized by the new federal Program for Social Innovation.

A Declaration Initiative should be designed to welcome to the Initiative's mission middle- and low-income citizens as well as interested wealthier participants. Private foundations are already spearheading inclusivity and many of the best approaches could be adapted to the Initiative challenges. Local giving circles, for instance—such as those sponsored by the Washington Women's Foundation or the Community Investment Network in North Carolina or any number of community foundations—operate as grassroots grant makers in their communities. The previously mentioned associations of African-American, Hispanic, Asian, and Native-American philanthropists across the nation are also natural allies. An engaging Declaration Initiative would attract these resources to join in the work on behalf of all citizens.

As we have learned through the wise philanthropy of Andrew Carnegie and Julius Rosenwald, every participating community must have "skin in the game." Rosenwald asked formerly enslaved sharecroppers to contribute to build a school for their children. He respected them as partners. Every improvement effort begins locally in the hearts of the people. Communities must want—maybe even choose—the improvement that will get foundation support. No outside philanthropist can simply deliver an asset and expect it will be well used, no matter how valuable. Olivia Sage found this out in Sag Harbor, New York, where her well-intentioned generosity was ultimately rejected by the community. Carnegie and Rosenwald acted as co-investors with communities. Neither arrived as Santa Claus delivering unexpected presents from the North Pole. Their stories offer important guiding principles to Initiative leaders, ones that could help ensure that local projects respect and engage grassroots commitments.

Finally, invitations should eventually go to retired citizens, students, and interested community members to volunteer to help the Initiative project near their communities. Engaging the widest possible range of participants in a shared moral ambition with the measurable specificity of the Declaration Initiative can only benefit our country and make the 2026 celebration more memorable.

Organize a Lean, Entrepreneurial Project Management Structure

The foundation sector has built a strong set of tools to continue strengthening its work. These tools will be critically important to the success of the Declaration Initiative. The philanthropic business-venture approach, focused on investment and hands-on engagement, has developed a number of model projects. The Fisher family's venture investment in the KIPP schools has created a national model of K–12 education. Venture Philanthropy Partners and others offer another kind of business-venture approach to social transformation that has scored remarkable successes. Hitachi's employee-led Community Action Committees provide another model and National Workforce Fund Solutions still another. Entrepreneurial philanthropy is all around and could unite around a common vision of achieving the Founders' intent by America's 250th Independence Day.

The work of many organizations suggests additional promising ways to identify needs and to create, monitor, and measure high-impact, evidenced-based social change.* Joel Fleishman reminds us that private foundations have scored successes using a variety of strategies, whether through driving change themselves, through partnerships, or as passive funders. Paul Brest offers context and a shared language for the work ahead. In addition, many university programs in social entrepreneurship are educating larger numbers of people ready to participate in and lead high-quality, productive, compassionate social change using tools and insights gleaned from our capital-market system. It is essential that the Declaration Initiative capture the energy, imagination, and technical expertise from every component of philanthropic leadership.†

Assure a Strong Communications Plan

Another important "how" includes a well-designed approach to announcing the Initiative, managing expectations, getting the word to all constituencies that can be expected to participate, and producing appropriate updates as the years progress. Widespread skepticism is currently very chic, so this communications plan will require discipline and depth so that the idealism of the Initiative is not trivialized and potentially undermined.

---

* I am thinking of Grantmakers for Effective Organizations (GEO), See Change, Caring for Change, Venture Philanthropy Partners (VPP), and Social Venture Partners (SVP), among others.

† I recognize that it is not appropriate to dive too deeply into details when providing food for thought. However, I cannot resist suggesting that such students might be engaged in local change efforts as part of their academic programs.

Chapter Eleven

In Due Time

As the early phases of planning evolve, a leadership team will want to begin creating sets of goals that appear possible at appropriate times during the fifteen-year sweep of the Initiative. These conveners will face the challenge of building buy-in across the spectrum of community and national constituencies. The key will be the discipline of maintaining focus on the goal of advancing the largest possible number of citizens to the well-being levels of the current middle class.

Whether planners focus on significant reductions in deaths among newborns or on increasing the numbers of households where children grow up with two married parents, or the many other promising pathways to middle-class growth, the key will be measurable progress to build momentum.

With the help of professionals in the field of assessment, the Initiative will need to develop an effective system to monitor progress and support faltering sites. The "how" of the Initiative sounds intimidating unless we remember the achievements of our nation. The Founders launched a new nation governed by the rule of law. All laws would apply equally to all citizens. More recently, Americans put a man on the moon and helped decode the human genome. The Initiative is ambitious, the stakes are high, and the impediments are mostly in our hands to mitigate.

Conclusion

Despite the economic crises and the reckless terrorists that confront us, Americans should establish a vision worthy of the 250th anniversary of the Founders' great work. Along with fireworks, barbecues, and bunting, we need a substantive initiative to celebrate the legacy we have received from our statesmen founders and our republican mothers. Our forebears would appreciate our work to end fatal disparities. Our children and grandchildren would see a reason to feel deeply patriotic.

Even if the fatal disparities could be eliminated or at least vastly reduced, poverty would survive. I understand that. But no one could say that Americans no longer take "all men are created equal" seriously. Moreover, many more Americans who are now lost to the community would be actively contributing as they enjoyed "life, liberty, and the pursuit of happiness." These are our first principles. As they initiated the creation of the Union, we could reassert them to reshape it to approximate more closely what most of the Founders envisioned.

I have no illusions that philanthropy alone can grow the middle class. However, our history suggests that profound improvements in social well-being and productivity have emerged from the citizen sector—the generous, idealistic, and private entrepreneurial sector in America. The imagination and the invitations need to take over where distrust and arrogance have begun to dominate. The failure of home ownership as the accepted strategy to middle-class stability has left a legacy of cynicism and disappointment. We need new ideas. We need all kinds of expertise, especially that of local community members and their leaders. This is a job that could reinvigorate American ideals.

Chapter Eleven

Many investors in the Declaration Initiative will be the children and grandchildren of what we call the Greatest Generation, as I am. My father, like his squadron members, was pilot, navigator, and gunner in his P-51. Having flown solo missions and been shot down and taken prisoner in Japan, he taught me, as many of my generation were taught, to believe that there was nothing I couldn't do if I set my mind to it. The Declaration Initiative is one way to envision, design, grit our teeth, and succeed at co-creating with our fellow Americans a future that would make our generation worthy scions of that Greatest Generation. In a skeptical age, this work could reanimate the idea of American exceptionalism for the twenty-first century.

The Theory of Change
For the Declaration Initiative[1]

The sustained engagement of foundation leaders (conservative, centrist, and liberal) on eliminating one or more of the fatal disparities that undermine the life, liberty, and pursuit of happiness of the poor would align philanthropic resources at all levels to reduce disparities and strengthen the U.S. economy.

This is a powerful approach that citizens can take to address the country's social and fiscal problems. Two kinds of infrastructure have developed. One has created solutions to disparities, and could stimulate others. Another fundraising infrastructure has evolved in an intricate network from the grassroots to community and national foundations.

Apparent Effectiveness

Large numbers of individual foundations from all three political sectors have achieved successful interventions with grantees dealing with elements of the fatal disparities. This experience gives them common ground, common grassroots connections, and the potential for common goals. Reviewing together more extensively evaluated programs may permit the local efforts to develop and fund more effective programs and evaluate them in terms of national goals.

Demonstrated Effectiveness

As the national Declaration Initiative would progress, projects demonstrating effectiveness would be available for replication in other areas of the country. The Initiative's assessment team would visit programs and projects and work with local philanthropic staffs and grassroots leaders to evaluate the effectiveness of the efforts to assure that the most effective interventions served the people.

Proven Effectiveness

Ultimately, as the Initiative moved forward along with other ongoing interventions on behalf of the poor, more broadly based evaluations of effectiveness might begin to establish best practices for addressing certain problems, like infant mortality, for instance. These developments during the ten to fifteen years of the Declaration Initiative would enable the philanthropic sector to more effectively enable local populations to avoid falling into fatal disparities in the future.

NOTES

INTRODUCTION

1. Many twenty-first-century studies confirm the value philanthropy brings to economic and social growth. Arthur Brooks notes several sources in his edited volume, *Gifts of Time and Money* (New York: Rowman and Littlefield, 2006). Among these are Mark Pomerantz, "The Business of Social Entrepreneurship in a 'Down Economy,'" *In Business* 23 (March 2003): 25–28; Sarah H. Alvord, L. David Brown, and Christine W. Letts, "Social Entrepreneurship and Societal Transformation: An Exploratory Study," *Journal of Applied Behavioral Science* 40, no. 3 (2004): 260–82.

CHAPTER ONE

1. The text and formal staff analysis of the bill can be found online at http://info.sen.ca.gov/cgi-bin/postquery?bill_number=ab_624&sess=PREV&house=B&site=sen.
2. Details of the agreement and links to various op-ed pieces commenting on it can be found online at http://www.nonprofitlawblog.com. See also the lengthy overview of what happened before, during, and after the AB 624 legislation by Rick Cohen, former director of NCRP, "Putting the AB 624 into Policy and Practice," http://racialequityblog.wordpress.com. While he does plenty of editorializing about the shortcomings of foundations in this area, Cohen provides a detailed accounting of the events.
3. Robert J. Shapiro and Aparna Mathur, *The Social and Economic Value of Private and Community Foundations* (Washington, D.C.: Philanthropic Collaborative, 2008).
4. The statistics for women, blacks, and the aged come from the U.S. Census Bureau at http://quickfacts.census.gov/qfd/states/00000.html. The gay and lesbian percentage is taken from http://www.urban.org/publications/1000491.html.
5. Naomi Schaefer Riley, "American Philanthropic Diversity: What It Means, Why It Matters" (monograph, Philanthropy Roundtable, March 2009).

6. Paul Brest, "NCRP at its Most Presumptuous," *Huffington Post*, March 5, 2009, http://www.huffingtonpost.com/paul-brest/ncrp-at-its-most-presumpt_b_172086.html.

7. Orson Aguilar, "Philanthropy's Race Problem," December 8, 2008, http://www.colorlines.com/article.php?ID=454.

8. Brest, "NCRP at its Most Presumptuous."

9. Aguilar, "Philanthropy's Race Problem."

CHAPTER TWO

1. Franklin Parker, *George Peabody, A Biography* (Nashville, TN: Vanderbilt University Press, 1995), 59.

2. Ibid., 192.

3. Ibid., 90.

4. Ibid., 82.

5. Ibid., 162.

6. Ibid., 192.

7. See Claire Gaudiani, *Generosity Rules!* (Bloomington, IN: IUniverse Press, 2007), 28.

8. Ibid.

9. Ibid., 34.

CHAPTER THREE

Epigraph: John Winthrop, "A Modell of Christian Charity" (1630), http://history.hanover.edu/texts/winthmod.htm. This is the first written text defining the philanthropic spirit in America.

1. Andrew Carnegie, *The Gospel of Wealth and Other Timely Essays* (New York: Century Club, 1901), 15. Cited by William Simon in "Challenges to Philanthropic Freedom," a speech presented to the Heritage Foundation on September 16, 2009. In his autobiography, Carnegie recounts challenging himself to act on these principles when, at age thirty-three, his income had already reached some $50,000 per year. See *The Autobiography of Andrew Carnegie* (Boston: Houghton Mifflin Company, 1920), 157–58.

2. Edwin J. Perkins, "The Entrepreneurial Spirit in Colonial America: The Foundations of Modern Business History," *Business History Review* 63, no. 1 (Spring 1989): 173.

3. Ibid., 186.

4. Bernard Bailyn, *Voyagers to the West: A Passage in the Peopling of America on the Eve of the Revolution* (New York: Knopf, 1986), 200.

5. Perkins, "The Entrepreneurial Spirit in Colonial America," 165.

6. Benjamin Franklin, *Writings* (New York: Library of America, 1987), 978–79.

7. From John Hope Franklin to Thomas G. West, the body of work on this subject by professional historians is vast, rich, and widely disparate in conclusions. See bibliography for recommended scholarly work on the intellectual origins of our nation.

8. Paul Finkelman—in *Slavery and the Founders: Race and Liberty in the Age of Jefferson*, 2nd ed. (New York: M. E. Sharpe, 2001)—addresses the intricacies of the legislative processes with particular skill and clarity.

9. This important subject deserves further exploration and the following works offer a starting point: Finkelman, *Slavery and the Founders*; Robert McColley, *Slavery and Jeffersonian Virginia* (Urbana: University of Illinois, 1964); Staughton Lynd, *Class Conflict, Slavery and the United States Constitution* (Indianapolis, IN: Bobbs Merrill, 1968); William Cohen, "Thomas Jefferson and the Problem of Slavery," *Journal of American History* 65 (1969): 503–26; Winthrop D. Jordan, *White over Black: American Attitudes Towards the Negro, 1550-1812* (Chapel Hill: University of North Carolina Press, 1968); Donald L. Robinson, *Slavery and the Structure of American Politics* (New York: Harcourt Brace Jovanovich, 1971); Robert A. Goldwin and Art Kaufman, *Slavery and Its Consequences* (Washington, D.C.: American Enterprise Institute, 1988); and Peter S. Onuf, ed., *Jeffersonian Legacies* (Charlottesville: University of Virginia Press, 1993).

10. William W. Freehling, "The Founding Fathers and Slavery," *American Historical Review* 77, no. 1 (February 1972): 82.

11. James D. Richardson, ed., *A Compilation of the Messages and Papers of the Presidents*, http://onlinebooks.library.upenn.edu/webbin/metabook?id=mppresidents.

12. Freehling, "The Founding Fathers and Slavery," 86.

13. Scot A. French and Edward L. Ayers, "The Strange Career of Thomas Jefferson: Race and Slavery in American Memory, 1943–1993," in *Jeffersonian Legacies*, 451.

14. David McCullough in a speech at DePauw University in 2002, online at http://www.depauw.edu/news/index.asp?id=11967.

15. Letter of Thomas Jefferson to James Madison, September 6, 1789, http://www.let.rug.nl/usa/P/tj3/writings/brf/jefl81.htm.

16. James Madison, "The Detached Memorandum," http://classicliberal.tripod.com/madison/detached4.html.

17. Bret Carroll, ed., *American Masculinities: A Historical Encyclopedia* (New York: Sage Publications, 2003), 411.

18. Bernard Bailyn, *The Ideological Origins of the American Revolution* (Cambridge, MA: Harvard University Press, 1967), 23.

19. Montesquieu's comment that republics differed from other political systems by the reliance they placed on virtue is explored in Howard Mumford Jones, *O Strange New World* (New York: Viking Press, 1964), 431.

20. Daniel Walker Howe, "Why the Scottish Enlightenment Was Useful to the Framers of the American Constitution," *Comparative Studies in Society and History* 31, no. 3 (July 1989): 576.

21. Adam Smith, *The Wealth of Nations* (Amherst, NY: Prometheus Books, 1991).
22. The exact source of this widely quoted assertion by Voltaire is not readily apparent.
23. Howe, 576.
24. Ibid., 580.
25. This fascinating and rich history has preoccupied researchers since at least 1907. Garry Wills wrote the brilliant and highly controversial *Inventing America: Jefferson's Declaration of Independence* and reinvigorated the topic among historians and interested citizens (Garry Wills, *Inventing America: Jefferson's Declaration of Independence* [Garden City, NY: Doubleday and Company, 1978]).
26. Abigail Adams, *My Dearest Friend: Letters of Abigail and John Adams*, ed. Margaret A. Hogan and C. James Taylor (Cambridge, MA: Belknap Press of Harvard University Press, 2007), 110.
27. Benjamin Rush, *Essays: Literary, Moral, and Philosophical* (Philadelphia: Thomas and Samuel Bradford, 1798), 6–7.
28. Quoted in Linda Kerber, *Toward an Intellectual History of Women* (Chapel Hill: University of North Carolina, 1997), 38–39. Additional quotes filled with equal enthusiasm are included by Kerber as well.
29. Judith Sargent Murray, *The Gleaner* (1798), 189. Murray was also the author of *On the Equality of the Sexes* (1792).
30. Kerber, *Toward an Intellectual History of Women*, 38–39.
31. See Ann F. Scott, *Natural Allies* (Chicago: University of Illinois Press, 1991).
32. Oliver Wendell Holmes, Jr., "Learning and Science," *Collected Legal Papers* (New York: Harcourt, Brace, and Howe, 1920), 139.

CHAPTER FOUR

Epigraph: Emmett Carson, "Current Challenges to Foundation Board Governance: A Worst Case Scenario or The Perfect Storm?" May 2003 Council on Foundations, http://www.cof.org/files/Documents/Speeches%20Important%20not%20CEO/carsonspeech42003.pdf.
1. For the appropriate references to the statutes involved, see Chris Abbinante, "Protecting Donor Intent: Wayward Trusteeship and the Barnes Foundation," *University of Pennsylvania Law Review* 145, no. 3 (January 1997): 679.
2. See http://foundationcenter.org/findfunders.
3. See *Chronicle of Philanthropy*, October 29, 2009, for additional details.
4. See Mark Rosenman, "Caring to Change: Foundations for the Common Good," slides seven through nine on pages 45–46, http://www.caringtochange.org/images/stories/C2C_Foundations_for_the_Common_Good.pdf.
5. Information on the preferences and motivations of the wealthy is of great business value to service providers such as money managers, insurance companies, legal advisors, and high-end retailers. For a basic bibliography, see Paul Schervish,

"Why the Wealthy Give," in *Routledge Companion to Nonprofit Marketing*, ed. Adrian Sergeant and Walter Wymer (New York: Routledge Publishers, 2008), 173–90.

6. See Theresa Odendahl, ed., *America's Wealthy and the Future of Foundations*, (New York: Foundation Center, 1987), 16–18.

7. Schervish, "Why the Wealthy Give."

8. Ibid., 179.

9. See Fleishman, *The Foundation*, 59–69, for a detailed discussion of these categories.

10. Described in Joel Fleishman, Scott Kohler, and Steven Schindler, *Casebook for The Foundation* (New York: Public Affairs, 2007), 259–63. The Edna McConnell Clark Foundation Youth Development Program illustrates the idea.

11. Shapiro and Mathur, *The Social and Economic Value of Private and Community Foundations*.

12. See http://www.ihaveadreamfoundation.org.

CHAPTER FIVE

Epigraph: Mary Douglas, quoted in Ruth Crocker, "From Gift to Foundation: The Philanthropic Lives of Mrs. Russell Sage," in *Charity, Philanthropy, and Civility in American History*, ed. Lawrence Friedman and Mark McGarvie (Cambridge: Cambridge University Press, 2003), 199.

1. The history of private foundations is long and rich. I do not pretend to do justice to the topic in this brief chapter. I highly recommend two readable and insightful sources. First, Joel Fleishman's book, *The Foundation*, previously cited, is complimented by its invaluable "casebook," mentioned above. A more analytical, scholarly view is available through the essays contained in *Charity, Philanthropy, and Civility in American History*.

2. For an engaging and thorough history of entrepreneurship, see David Pozen, "We Are All Entrepreneurs Now," *Wake Forest Law Journal* 43 (2008): 287–98.

3. Quoted in Eleanor Brilliant, *Private Charity and Public Inquiry* (Bloomington: Indiana University Press, 2000), 19.

4. The Treasurer's Papers of Yale University (December 1831), quoted by the author, *The Greater Good* (New York: Henry Holt, 2003), 36.

5. A brief summary and bibliography for this work is found in Fleishman's *Casebook for The Foundation,* 39–42.

6. *The Greater Good*, 112.

7. For a more complete discussion of philanthropy during this era, see David Hammack, "Failure and Resilience," in Friedman and McGarvie, 263–80.

8. The Elizabethan Statute of Charitable Uses of 1601.

9. The full story of the development decade is told in chapter fifteen of Friedman and McGarvie, "Waging the Cold War in the Third World," by Gary Hess.

10. It is of course impossible to do justice to the impact of Soros's work in a few short sentences. For starters, I recommend Michael Kaufman, *Soros: The Life and Times of a Messianic Billionaire* (New York: Knopf, 2002).

11. See http://www.lauderfoundation.com for additional information country by country.

12. See Odendahl, *American's Wealthy and the Future of Foundations*. The studies were funded by Kellogg, Mellon, and Mott foundations.

13. See Mike Spector, "Family Charities Shift Assets to Donor-Advised Funds," *Wall Street Journal*, April 22, 2009.

14. See the Cleveland Foundation Web site at http://clevelandfoundation.org.

15. See http://www.wingsweb.org for the details.

16. See "SSIR Managing Editor Eric Nee Interviews Emmett Carson," *Stanford Social Innovation Review* (Summer 2007). Full text available online at http://www.siliconvalleycf.org/docs/2007SU_15minutes_carson.pdf.

17. See the thoughtful 2005 piece by William H. Hewitt, "Are We There Yet? Is the Financial Services Industry Ready for Donor Advised Funds?" available online at http://blackbaud.com under the section "Kintera white papers."

18. Ibid.

CHAPTER SIX

Epigraph: Robert Goheen, former president of Princeton University, quoted by Peter Hall, "The Welfare State," in Friedman and McGarvie, 363.

1. The following sources are recommended for additional reading: Eleanor Brilliant's *Private Charity and Public Inquiry*, Peter Hall's "The Welfare State" in Friedman and McGarvie, and Theresa Odendahl's *America's Wealthy and the Future of Foundations*.

2. See Ellen P. Aprill, "Churches, Politics and the Charitable Contribution Deduction," *Boston College Law Review* 42, no. 4 (2001): 843–74. Aprill notes that the primary reason for the inclusion of the deduction was concern that contributions to higher education, which Senator Henry Hollis (R-NH) noted were almost entirely dependent on private generosity, might drop precipitously with the imposition of income taxes on the wealthiest taxpayers.

3. For a clear explanation of the history of this complex issue, see Jessica Peña and Alexander Reid, "A Call for Reform of the Operational Test for Unrelated Commercial Activities in Charities," *New York University Law Review* 76, no. 6 (November 2001): 1856–96.

4. Cited by Brilliant, 71.

5. Ibid., 45.

6. The Independent Sector (http://www.independentsector.org) has a helpful overview of these regulations as well as links to current IRS guidance for not-for-profits. For an illustration of the complexity of this area, see J. A. Kerlin

and E. J. Reid, "The Financing and Programming of Advocacy in Complex Nonprofit Structures," *Nonprofit and Voluntary Sector Quarterly* 38, no. 3 (June 2009).

7. Brilliant, 124.

8. Ibid., 126.

9. For a complete listing, see Marion Fremont-Smith, *Foundations and Government: State and Federal Law and Supervision* (New York: Russell Sage Foundation, 1965), 41.

10. Susan Gary, "UMIFA Becomes UPMIFA," published by the Uniform Law Commission and available online at http://www.nccusl.org/nccusl/Docs/ UMIFA%20Becomes%20UPMIFA.pdf.

11. The reforms are detailed by the Council of Foundations at http://www.cof.org.

CHAPTER SEVEN

Epigraph: Thomas Jefferson, *Letter to James Madison*, September 6, 1789, http://www. let.rug.nl/usa/P/tj3/writings/brf/jefl81.htm. William Robertson, "Donor Intent Revisited," *Washington Times*, September 28, 2008. Robert Bork, "Interpreting the Founder's Vision," *Philanthropic Prospect* (Washington, D.C.: Philanthropy Round-table, 1993), 13. Andrew Carnegie, cited in Fleishman, *The Foundation*, 291.

1. Recommended for additional reading are the following three titles from Marion Fremont-Smith: *Governing Nonprofit Organizations: Federal and State Law and Regula-tion* (Cambridge, MA: Harvard University Press, 2004); *Foundations and Govern-ment: State and Federal Law and Supervision*; and "Holding the Tension: History and Policy," a paper presented at the National Center on Philanthropy conference "Grasping the Nettle: Respecting Donor Intent and Avoiding the Dead Hand." For an advocacy position supporting respect for donor intent, see Martin Morse Wooster, *The Great Philanthropists and the Problem of Donor Intent* (Washington, D.C.: Capital Research Center, 2008). For the question of perpetuity versus limited-term or spend-down foundations, see Lori Lenz and David Wolcheck, *Perpe-tuity or Limited Lifespan* (monograph, The Foundation Center, 2009), http:// foundationcenter.org/gainknowledge/research/pdf/perpetuity2009.pdf

2. Fremont-Smith, "Holding the Tension."

3. See Abbinante, "Protecting Donor Intent," 681–83, for the relevant legal cases that have contributed to the development of *cy pres* and deviation.

4. The role of the attorney general in the enforcement of donor intent has been a subject of debate. See Marion Fremont-Smith, "Attorney General Oversight of Charities," Hauser Center for Nonprofit Organizations, Harvard Univer-sity, Working Paper #41 (October 1997), http://www.hks.harvard.edu/hauser/ PDF_XLS/workingpapers/workingpaper_41.pdf.

5. See Evelyn Brody, "From the Dead Hand to the Living Dead," *Georgia Law Review* 41 (2007): 1183–276.

6. Kathryn Miree and Winston Smith, "The Unraveling of Donor Intent: Lawsuits and Lessons," available online through the Planned Giving Design Center at http://www.pgdc.com.

7. For the San Francisco Foundation perspective, see Martin A. Paley, "The Challenge of the Buck Trust," *Threepenny Review* 18 (Summer 1984): 15–20.

8. See Stephanie Strom, "Not All of Helmsley's Trust Has to Go to Dogs," *New York Times*, February 25, 2009.

9. For a critique of Posner's argument, see Abbinante, "Protecting Donor Intent," 697.

10. Bork, "Interpreting the Founder's Vision."

11. Curtis W. Meadows, Jr., "Philanthropic Choice and Donor Intent: Freedom, Responsibility and Public Interest," presented in the Waldemar A. Nielsen Issues in Philanthropy Seminar Series at Georgetown University, November 22, 2002, http://cpnl.georgetown.edu/doc_pool/Nielsen0205Meadows.pdf. Meadows is himself a longtime foundation trustee, philanthropic advisor, lawyer, and benefactor.

12. Waldemar Nielsen, "The Donor's Role in Donor Intent," *Donor Intent*, (Washington, D.C.: Philanthropic Prospect, 1992), 19.

13. See Fleishman, *The Foundation*, chapter fourteen.

14. See note eight, chapter six.

15. Meadows, 2.

CHAPTER EIGHT

1. Pablo Eisenberg, "What's Wrong with Charitable Giving and How to Fix It," *Wall Street Journal*, November 9, 2009.

2. See Mark Rosenman, "Caring to Change: Foundations for the Common Good," http://www.caringtochange.org/images/stories/C2C_Foundations_for_the_Common_Good.pdf, 3.

3. See http://www.philanthropyawareness.org.

4. Paul Brest and Hal Harvey, *Money Well Spent* (New York: Bloomberg Press, 2008).

5. The Center for Effective Philanthropy (http://www.effectivephilanthropy.org) provides such evaluative services to foundations. It interviews and surveys grant recipients on a wide range of questions and aggregates data so that anonymity is maintained for participants. The Bridgespan Group (http://www.bridgespan.org) has also created a large database of recipients' feedback for foundations.

6. Fleishman, *The Foundation*, quoted by Mario Morino, "Chairman's Corner" (September 2009), http://www.vppartners.org/learning/perspectives/corner/0909_here-comes-the-sun.html.

7. See also Marion Fremont-Smith and Andras Kosaras, "Wrongdoing by Officers and Directors of Charities," Hauser Center for Nonprofit Organizations, Har-

vard University, Working Paper #20 (September 2003), http://www.sos.state.co.us/pubs/charities/char_fraud_art_wrongdoing.pdf.

8. Eisenberg, "What's Wrong with Charitable Giving and How to Fix It."

9. Mario Morino, "Transparency Revolution," December 8, 2009, http://cspcs.sanford.duke.edu/blog/morino_transparency_revolution.

10. See Mary Oates, "Faith and Good Works: Catholic Giving and Taking," in Friedman and McGarvie, 281–99.

CHAPTER NINE

Epigraph: Glenn C. Loury, "The Economics of Racial Equality and Justice," in *Faithful Economics*, ed. John Pisciotta and James W. Henderson (Waco, TX: Baylor University Press, 2005), 54.

1. Carolyn Adams, "The Meds and Eds in Urban Economic Development," *Journal of Urban Affairs* 25, no. 5 (December 2003): 571–88.

2. See http://aspe.hhs.gov/hsp/09/philanpart/chapter1.shtml#_ftn4.

3. Brest and Harvey, *Money Well Spent*.

CHAPTER TEN

Epigraph: Bishop Richard Allen, *Freedom's Journal*, 1827.

1. M. A. H. Hargraves, *The Social Construction of Infant Mortality: From Grass Roots to Medicalization*, thesis (Houston: University of Texas Health Science Center, 1992).

2. The mortality risk ratio for 1,000 babies born to black mothers with little education was 1.9 (i.e., almost twice as great) when compared with college-educated black mothers and 3.9 (i.e., almost four times greater) when compared with college-educated white mothers. See C. J. R. Hogue, et. al., "Overview of the national infant mortality surveillance (NIMS): project design, methods, results," *Public Health Report* 102, no. 2 (March/April 1987): 126–38.

3. See Todd Risley and Betty Hart, *Meaningful Differences in the Everyday Experiences of Young American Children* (Baltimore: Brookes Publishing, 1995). Risley and Hart document the wide differences in vocabulary size and IQ scores between poor children and those raised in higher-income households. These deficiencies correlate powerfully with future lack of success in school. Researchers found the strongest influence on a student's vocabulary was the type of talk children participated in as infants, toddlers, and preschoolers. The number of words that children knew at age three was found to be predictive of achievement at age nine. However, some children of well-educated parents who didn't spend much time talking with their children had similar average minutes of verbal interaction as some welfare and working-class families. Across the board, the researchers found that race did not influence vocabulary.

4. See the Gerald R. Ford School of Public Policy at the University of Michigan, National Poverty Center, http://www.npc.umich.edu/poverty/#3.

5. U.S. Bureau of the Census, "Income, Poverty, and Health Insurance Coverage in the United States: 2008, Report P60," n. 236, table B-2, 50–55.

6. Harry J. Holzer, et. al., "The Economic Costs of Poverty in the United States: Subsequent Effects of Children Growing Up Poor," Center For American Progress (January 24, 2007), http://www.americanprogress.org/issues/2007/01/pdf/poverty_report.pdf.

7. Ibid.

8. Ibid.

9. Gabor Steingart, *War for Wealth: The True Story of Globalization, Or Why the Flat World is Broken* (New York: McGraw Hill, 2008).

10. Fareed Zakaria, "The Rise of the Rest," *Newsweek*, May 12, 2008.

11. James Fallows, "How America Can Rise Again," *Atlantic Monthly,* January/February 2010.

12. Niall Ferguson, *Foreign Affairs*, March/April 2010: 18–32.

CHAPTER ELEVEN

1. See Paul Brest, "The Power of Theories of Change," *Stanford Social Innovation Review* (Spring 2010): 46.

BIBLIOGRAPHY

Abbinante, Chris. "Protecting Donor Intent: Wayward Trusteeship and the Barnes Foundation." *University of Pennsylvania Law Review* 145, no. 3 (January 1997).

Adams, Abigail. *My Dearest Friend: Letters of Abigail and John Adams.* Edited by Margaret A. Hogan and C. James Taylor. Cambridge, MA: Belknap Press of Harvard University Press, 2007.

Adams, Carolyn. "The Meds and Eds in Urban Economic Development." *Journal of Urban Affairs* 25, no. 5 (December 2003): 571–88.

Aguilar, Orson. "Philanthropy's Race Problem." December 8, 2008, http://www.colorlines.com/article.php?ID=454.

Alvord, Sarah H., L. David Brown, and Christine W. Letts. "Social Entrepreneurship and Societal Transformation: An Exploratory Study." *Journal of Applied Behavioral Science* 40, no. 3 (2004): 260–82.

Aprill, Ellen P. "Churches, Politics and the Charitable Contribution Deduction." *Boston College Law Review* 42, no. 4 (2001): 843–74.

Bailyn, Bernard. *The Ideological Origins of the American Revolution.* Cambridge, MA: Harvard University Press, 1967.

——— *Voyagers to the West: A Passage in the Peopling of America on the Eve of the Revolution.* New York: Knopf, 1986.

Becerra, Xavier. Editorial. *Wall Street Journal*, December 24, 2008.

Bergengren, Roy. *Credit Union North America.* New York: Southern Publishers, 1940.

Blankenhorn, David. *Thrift: A Cyclopedia.* West Conshohocken, PA: Templeton Press, 2007.

Blinderman, Abraham. *Three Early Champions of Education.* Bloomington: Indiana University Press, 1976.

Bork, Robert. "Interpreting the Founder's Vision." *Philanthropic Prospect.* Washington, D.C.: Philanthropy Roundtable, 1993.

Brest, Paul. "NCRP at its Most Presumptuous." *Huffington Post*, March 5, 2009, http://www.huffingtonpost.com/paul-brest/ncrp-at-its-most-presumpt_b_172086.html.

———— and Hal Harvey. *Money Well Spent*. New York: Bloomberg Press, 2008.

———— "The Power of Theories of Change." *Stanford Social Innovation Review* (Spring 2010).

Brilliant, Eleanor. *Private Charity and Public Inquiry*. Bloomington: Indiana University Press, 2000.

Brody, Evelyn, and John Tyler, "How Public Is Private Philanthropy? Separating Myth from Reality." Monograph, Philanthropy Roundtable, 2009.

Brooks, Arthur, ed. *Gifts of Time and Money*. New York: Rowman and Littlefield, 2006.

Burke, Edmund. *Reflections on the Revolution in France*. London: J. M. Dent and Sons, 1955.

Carnegie, Andrew. *The Gospel of Wealth and Other Timely Essays*. New York: Century Club, 1901.

———— *The Autobiography of Andrew Carnegie*. Boston: Houghton Mifflin Company, 1920.

Carroll, Bret, ed. *American Masculinities: A Historical Encyclopedia*. New York: Sage Publications, 2003.

Carson, Emmett. "Current Challenges to Foundation Board Governance: A Worst Case Scenario or The Perfect Storm?" Council on Foundations, May 2003, http://www.cof.org/files/Documents/Speeches%20Important%20not%20CEO/carsonspeech42003.pdf

Cohen, Rick. "Putting the AB 624 into Policy and Practice," http://racialequityblog.wordpress.com.

Cohen, William. "Thomas Jefferson and the Problem of Slavery." *Journal of American History* 65 (1969): 503–26.

Crocker, Ruth. *Mrs. Russell Sage*. Bloomington: Indiana University Press, 2006.

Department of Health and Human Services. "Maximizing the Value of Philanthropic Efforts through Planned Partnerships between the U.S. Government and Private Foundations," http://aspe.hhs.gov/hsp/09/philanpart/chapter1.shtml#_ftn4.

Duncan, George John C. *Memoir of the Rev. Henry Duncan, D.D. of Ruthwell*. Edinburgh: William Oliphant and Sons, 1848.

Bibliography

Eisenberg, Pablo. "What's Wrong with Charitable Giving and How to Fix It." *Wall Street Journal*, November 9, 2009.

Esty, Katharine, Richard Griffin, and Marcie Schorr Hirsh. *Workplace Diversity: A Manager's Guide to Solving Problems and Turning Diversity into a Competitive Advantage*. Holbrook, MA: Adams Media Corporation, 1995.

Fallows, James. "How America Can Rise Again?" *Atlantic Monthly*, January/February 2010.

Ferguson, Niall. "Complexity and Collapse: Empires on the Edge of Chaos." *Foreign Affairs*. March/April 2010: 18–32.

Finkelman, Paul. *Slavery and the Founders: Race and Liberty in the Age of Jefferson*, 2nd ed. New York: M. E. Sharpe, 2001.

Fleishman, Joel. *The Foundation: A Great American Secret*, 2nd ed. New York: Public Affairs, 2009.

——— Scott Kohler, and Steven Schindler. *Casebook for The Foundation*. New York: Public Affairs, 2007.

Foundation Center. "Diversity in Philanthropy: A Comprehensive Bibliography of Resources Related to Diversity Within the Philanthropic and Nonprofit Sectors," http://foundationcenter.org/getstarted/topical/diversity.html.

Franklin, Benjamin. *Writings*. New York: Library of America, 1987.

Freehling, William W. "The Founding Fathers and Slavery." *American Historical Review* 77, no. 1 (February 1972): 81–93.

Fremont-Smith, Marion. "Attorney General Oversight of Charities," Hauser Center for Nonprofit Organizations, Harvard University, Working Paper #41 (October 1997), http://www.hks.harvard.edu/hauser/PDF_XLS/workingpapers/workingpaper_41.pdf.

——— *Foundations and Government: State and Federal Law and Supervision*. New York: Russell Sage Foundation, 1965.

——— *Governing Nonprofit Organizations: Federal and State Law and Regulation*. Cambridge, MA: Harvard University Press, 2004.

——— "Holding the Tension: History and Policy," a paper presented at the National Center on Philanthropy conference "Grasping the Nettle: Respecting Donor Intent and Avoiding the Dead Hand."

——— and Andras Kosaras, "Wrongdoing by Officers and Directors of Charities," Hauser Center for Nonprofit Organizations, Harvard University, Working Paper #20 (September 2003), http://www.sos.state.co.us/pubs/charities/char_fraud_art_wrongdoing.pdf.

Friedman, Lawrence, and Mark McGarvie, eds. *Charity, Philanthropy, and Civility in American History*. Cambridge: Cambridge University Press, 2003.

Gary, Susan. Letter to the Editor. *Chronicle of Philanthropy*, October 15, 2009.

———— "UMIFA becomes UPMIFA." Uniform Law Commission, http://www. nccusl.org/nccusl/Docs/UMIFA%20Becomes%20UPMIFA.pdf.

Gaudiani, Claire. *The Greater Good*. New York: Henry Holt, 2003.

———— *Generosity Rules!* Bloomington, IN: IUniverse Press, 2007.

Goldwin, Robert A., and Art Kaufman. *Slavery and Its Consequences*. Washington, D.C.: American Enterprise Institute, 1988.

Gouge, William. *A Learned Commentary on the Whole Epistle to the Hebrews*, http://www. puritanboard.com.

Hanley, Ryan Patrick. "Social Science and Human Flourishing: The Scottish Enlightenment and Today." *Journal of Scottish Philosophy* 7, no. 1 (2009): 29–46.

Hargraves, M. A. H. *The Social Construction of Infant Mortality: From Grass Roots to Medicalization*. Thesis, Houston: University of Texas Health Science Center, 1992.

Hewitt, William H. "Are We There Yet? Is the Financial Services Industry Ready for Donor Advised Funds?" http://blackbaud.com under the section "Kintera white papers."

Hogue, C. J. R., et. al. "Overview of the national infant mortality surveillance (NIMS): project design, methods, results." *Public Health Report* 102, no. 2 (March/April 1987): 126–38.

Holmes, Jr., Oliver Wendell. *Collected Legal Papers*. New York: Harcourt, Brace, and Howe, 1920.

Holzer, Harry J., et. al. "The Economic Costs of Poverty in the United States: Subsequent Effects of Children Growing Up Poor." Center For American Progress (January 24, 2007), http://www.americanprogress.org/issues/2007/01/pdf/ poverty_report.pdf.

Howe, Daniel Walker. "Why the Scottish Enlightenment Was Useful to the Framers of the American Constitution." *Comparative Studies in Society and History* 31, no. 3 (July 1989): 572–591.

Hubbard, Edward E. *The Diversity Scorecard: Evaluating the Impact of Diversity on Organizational Performance*. Oxford: Elsevier, 2004.

Hyde, Lewis. "Advantage Google." *New York Times Book Review*, October 4, 2009.

Isaacson, Walter. *Benjamin Franklin: An American Life*. New York: Simon and Schuster, 2003.

Bibliography

Jefferson, Thomas. Letter to James Madison, September 6, 1789, http://www.let.rug.nl/usa/P/tj3/writings/brf/jefl81.htm.

Jones, Howard Mumford. *O Strange New World*. New York: Viking Press, 1964.

Jordan, Winthrop D. *White over Black: American Attitudes Towards the Negro, 1550–1812*. Chapel Hill: University of North Carolina Press, 1968.

Kaufman, Michael. *Soros: The Life and Times of a Messianic Billionaire*. New York: Knopf, 2002.

Kerber, Linda K. *No Constitutional Right to Be Ladies*. New York: Hill and Wang, 1999.

———— *Toward an Intellectual History of Women*. Chapel Hill: University of North Carolina, 1997.

Kerlin, J. A., and E. J. Reid, "The Financing and Programming of Advocacy in Complex Nonprofit Structures." *Nonprofit and Voluntary Sector Quarterly* 38, no. 3 (June 2009).

Lenkowsky, Leslie. "In Philanthropy, It's Not Just About the Numbers." *Chronicle of Philanthropy*, January 29, 2009.

———— "Irving Kristol's Legacy for Philanthropy." *Chronicle of Philanthropy*, September 21, 2009.

Lenz, Lori, and David Wolcheck. "Perpetuity or Limited Lifespan." Monograph, Foundation Center, 2009, http://foundationcenter.org/gainknowledge/research/pdf/perpetuity2009.pdf

Loury, Glenn C. "The Economics of Racial Equality and Justice." *Faithful Economics*. Edited by John Pisciotta and James W. Henderson. Waco, TX: Baylor University Press, 2005.

Lynd, Staughton. *Class Conflict, Slavery and the United States Constitution*. Indianapolis, IN: Bobbs Merrill, 1968.

McColley, Robert. *Slavery and Jeffersonian Virginia*. Urbana: University of Illinois, 1964.

McCullough, David. Speech at DePauw University (2002), http://www.depauw.edu/news/index.asp?id=11967.

Meadows, Jr., Curtis W. "Philanthropic Choice and Donor Intent: Freedom, Responsibility and Public Interest," presented in the Waldemar A Nielsen Issues in Philanthropy Seminar Series at Georgetown University, November 22, 2002, http://cpnl.georgetown.edu/doc_pool/Nielsen0205Meadows.pdf.

Miree, Kathryn, and Winston Smith. "The Unraveling of Donor Intent: Lawsuits and Lessons," http://www.pgdc.com.

Montesquieu, Charles Louis Secondat, Baron de. *The Spirit of the Laws.* Cambridge: Cambridge University Press, 1989.

Morino, Mario. "Chairman's Corner." September 2009, http://www.vppartners.org/learning/perspectives/corner/0909_here-comes-the-sun.html.

——— "Transparency Revolution." December 8, 2009, http://cspcs.sanford.duke.edu/blog/morino_transparency_revolution.

Murray, Judith Sargent. *The Gleaner* (Boston: L. Thomas and E. T. Andrews, 1798).

National Council for Responsible Philanthropy. "Philanthropy at Its Best." Monograph, Washington, D.C., 2009.

National League of Cities. "*Poverty and Economic Insecurity: Views from City Hall,*" http://www.nlc.org/ASSETS/D6A52A2214A84F1EA208A18CDA25D83D/ExecutiveSummary.pdf.

National Poverty Center, Gerald R. Ford School of Public Policy at the University of Michigan. "Poverty in the United States, Frequently Asked Questions," http://www.npc.umich.edu/poverty/#3.

Nee, Eric. "SSIR Managing Editor Eric Nee Interviews Emmett Carson." *Stanford Social Innovation Review* (Summer 2007), http://www.siliconvalleycf.org/docs/2007SU_15minutes_carson.pdf.

Nielsen, Waldemar A. "The Donor's Role in Donor Intent." *Donor Intent.* Washington, D.C.: Philanthropic Prospect, 1992.

Odendahl, Theresa, ed. *America's Wealthy and the Future of Foundations.* New York: Foundation Center, 1987.

Onuf, Peter S., ed. *Jeffersonian Legacies.* Charlottesville: University of Virginia Press, 1993.

Paley, Martin A. "The Challenge of the Buck Trust." *Threepenny Review* 18 (Summer 1984): 15–20.

Parker, Franklin. *George Peabody, A Biography.* Nashville: Vanderbilt University Press, 1995.

Peña, Jessica, and Alexander Reid. "A Call for Reform of the Operational Test for Unrelated Commercial Activities in Charities." *New York University Law Review* 76, no. 6 (November 2001): 1856–96.

Perkins, Edwin J. "The Entrepreneurial Spirit in Colonial America: The Foundations of Modern Business History." *Business History Review* 63, no. 1 (Spring 1989): 160–186.

Pomerantz, Mark. "The Business of Social Entrepreneurship in a 'Down Economy.'" *In Business* 23 (March 2003): 25–28.

Bibliography

Pozen, David. "We Are All Entrepreneurs Now." *Wake Forest Law Journal* 43 (2008): 287–98.

Risley, Todd, and Betty Hart. *Meaningful Differences in the Everyday Experiences of Young American Children.* Baltimore: Brookes Publishing, 1995.

Reich, Rob. "A Failure of Philanthropy." *Stanford Social Innovation Review* (Winter 2005): 24–33.

Richardson, James D., ed. *A Compilation of the Messages and Papers of the Presidents,* http://onlinebooks.library.upenn.edu/webbin/metabook?id=mppresidents.

Riley, Naomi Schaefer. "American Philanthropic Diversity: What It Means, Why It Matters." Monograph, Philanthropy Roundtable, March 2009.

Robinson, Donald L. *Slavery and the Structure of American Politics.* New York: Harcourt Brace Jovanovich, 1971.

Rosenman, Mark. "Caring to Change: Foundations for the Common Good," http://www.caringtochange.org/images/stories/C2C_Foundations_for_the_Common_Good.pdf.

Rush, Benjamin. *Essays: Literary, Moral, and Philosophical.* Philadelphia: Thomas and Samuel Bradford, 1798.

Schervish, Paul. "Why the Wealthy Give," in *Routledge Companion to Nonprofit Marketing.* Edited by Adrian Sergeant and Walter Wymer. New York: Routledge Publishers, 2008.

Scott, Ann F. *Natural Allies.* Chicago: University of Illinois Press, 1991.

Shapiro, Robert J., and Aparna Mathur. *The Social and Economic Value of Private and Community Foundations.* Washington, D.C.: Philanthropic Collaborative, 2008.

Simon, William. "Challenges to Philanthropic Freedom." Presented to the Heritage Foundation, September 16, 2009, www.blog.heritage.org.

Smith, Adam. *The Wealth of Nations.* Amherst, NY: Prometheus Books, 1991.

——— *Theory of Moral Sentiments.* New York: Cosimo Books, 2007.

Spector, Mike. "Family Charities Shift Assets to Donor-Advised Funds." *Wall Street Journal,* April 22, 2009.

Stockdale, Margaret S., and Faye J. Crosby, eds. *The Psychology and Management of Workplace Diversity.* Malden, MA: Blackwell Publishing, 2004.

Strom, Stephanie. "Not All of Helmsley's Trust Has to Go to Dogs." *New York Times,* February 25, 2009.

Sullivan, Leon. "From Protest to Progress: The Lessons of the OIC." *Yale Law and Public Policy Review* 4, no. 2 (1986): 364–74.

Tocqueville, Alexis de. *Democracy in America*. Translated by Francis Bowen. Cambridge, MA: Sever and Francis, 1868.

Trevor-Roper, Hugh. "The Scottish Enlightenment." *Studies on Voltaire and the 18th Century* 68 (1967): 1635–58.

U.S. Bureau of the Census. "Income, Poverty, and Health Insurance Coverage in the United States: 2008, Report P60."

Wills, Garry. *Inventing America: Jefferson's Declaration of Independence*. Garden City, NY: Doubleday and Company, 1978.

Winthrop, John. "A Modell of Christian Charity," 1630, http://history.hanover.edu/texts/winthmod.htm.

Wooster, Martin Morse. *The Great Philanthropists and the Problem of Donor Intent*. Washington, D.C.: Capital Research Center, 2008.

Zakaria, Fareed, *The Post–American World*. New York: W. W. Norton, 2008.

———— "The Rise of the Rest." *Newsweek*, May 12, 2008.

INDEX

Index

Index

Index

Index

Index

United Kingdom, 193
United Negro College Fund, 51–52, 123
United Way, 103, 192
University Development Program, 134
University of Bologna, 66
University of California, 26, 129
University of Cambridge, 66
University of Chicago, 128
University of Edinburgh, 72
University of Michigan, 129, 131
University of Mississippi, 49–50
University of Oxford, 66
University of Paris, 66
University of Pennsylvania Law Review, 176n
University of Texas, 129, 179
University of Washington, 131
University of Wisconsin, 129
Unrelated Business Income Tax (UBIT) (1954), 153
US Commission on Industrial Relations
see Walsh Commission
US Steel, 111

V
Vanderbilt, Cornelius, 32
Vanderbilt University, 32, 35, 174
Vanguard, 101, 145
Venture Philanthropy Partners, 193, 235, 236n
Verne, Jules, 67
Vietnam War, 156
Villanueva, Danny Sr., 163
Virginia, 72
Voltaire (Francois Marie Arouet), 79

W
Wal-Mart, 137
Wald, Lillian, 28, 194
Wall Street Journal, 6n, 159, 188n
Walsh Commission, 151
Walton Foundation, 137
War of 1812, 30
War Reform Act (1917), 151
Washington, 104
Washington, George, 72
Washington Women's Foundation, 234
Watergate, 157
Watson, James, 129
Watt, James, 78, 79
"We Shall Overcome," 61
Wealth of Nations (Smith), 75
Weaver, Warren, 129
West Point, xvi
"What's Wrong with Charitable Giving and How to Fix It" (Eisenberg), 188n
Williams College, 188
Winfrey, Oprah, 21, 46–47, 163
Winston-Salem Community Foundation, 145
Winthrop, John, 54, 56–57, 57n
Wisconsin, 137
Witherspoon, John, 72–73, 75
Woodrow Wilson School, 173
Wooster, Martin, 176n, 180n
Workplace Diversity (Esty, Griffin, Hirsch), 15n
World Bank, 9n
World War I, 128, 130
World War II, 129, 133–35
Wren, Christopher, 66